Assessing Student Achievement

A Guide for Teachers and Administrators

Christopher Deneen and James Deneen

ROWMAN & LITTLEFIELD EDUCATION
Lanham • New York • Toronto • Plymouth, UK

Published in the United States of America
by Rowman & Littlefield Education
A Division of Rowman & Littlefield Publishers, Inc.
A wholly owned subsidary of The Rowman & Littlefield Publishing Group, Inc.
4501 Forbes Boulevard, Suite 200, Lanham, Maryland 20706
www.rowmaneducation.com

Estover Road
Plymouth PL6 7PY
United Kingdom

British Library Cataloguing in Publication Information Available

Library of Congress Cataloging-in-Publication Data

Deneen, Christopher, 1970–
    Assessing student achievement : a guide for teachers and administrators/
Christopher Deneen and James Deneen.
        p. cm.
    Includes bibliographical references.
    ISBN-13: 978-1-57886-809-4 (cloth : alk. paper)
    ISBN-10: 1-57886-809-2 (cloth : alk. paper)
    ISBN-13: 978-1-57886-810-0 (pbk. : alk. paper)
    ISBN-10: 1-57886-810-6 (pbk. : alk. paper)
    1. Students—Rating of—United States. 2. Academic achievement—United
States—Evaluation. 3. Educational tests and measurements—United States—
Evaluation. I. Deneen, James R. II. Title.
    LB3051.D434 2008
    371.26'4—dc22   2008002333

∞™ The paper used in this publication meets the minimum requirements of
American National Standard for Information Sciences—Permanence of Paper for
Printed Library Materials, ANSI/NISO Z39.48-1992.
Manufactured in the United States of America.

We dedicate this book to our beloved wife and mother, Thalia Stathas Deneen.

Contents

Preface

OUR PURPOSE

"Assess for Success" may be a bit too facile a slogan, but our intent in this book is to help teachers help their students succeed in school. Let's assume that the main, although not the sole, purpose of schooling in elementary, middle, and high school grades is to assist students in mastering the knowledge, skills, and attitudes they will need for further learning and for their adult lives. That mastery will depend heavily on the curriculum, that is, on what is taught.

We argue that the purpose of teaching is student learning, and that learning cannot be verified or even achieved without the proper use of student assessment. Our purpose in writing this book is to set a context for this thesis and explore it though presenting the basics of good assessment practices.

It's not news that some people believe that formally assessing students, especially through standardized tests, is counterproductive. The many alleged flaws of formal assessment include the following:

- They induce extreme anxiety in students and parents.
- They promote unhealthy competition among students (and parents).
- They waste time that could better be used for classroom instruction.

All assessments have flaws, and some have many flaws. We suggest, though, that the fault lies not in attempting to assess students, but in improper planning, adminstering, and using of assessment results. Another critical purpose of this book, then, is to describe some common errors committed assessment and suggest possible remedies. We will explain what constitutes appropriate standards and point out how classroom and standardized assessments that meet those standards serve important purposes.

Assessment should do more than provide a score or grade to students. How can the teacher and administrator increase the usefulness of assessment beyond assigning a number or letter to them? Some helpful uses of assessment are:

- Diagnosing student learning and deciding what individuals and the class as a whole need to learn next.
- Communicating student achievement to members of an educational community, such as the students and their parents.
- Highlighting the most important knowledge and skills that students need to master.
- Motivating students to extend and expand their learning.
- Helping to place students at appropriate grade levels.
- Measuring the effectiveness of instruction. This area has at least two elements: aiding teachers and administrators in perceiving when and how to modify their curricula, and providing insights into the school's success in meeting state and local standards of achievement.

The importance of assessment in these professional tasks emphasizes our intent in writing this book. We want to give teachers and administrators in grades K–12 a *practical* guide to assessment; that is, we want to show how teachers can use assessment to further their goals for student learning. This text is directed primarily to classroom teachers and administrators, roles both authors have filled, and one of us continues to play. We introduce many examples of classroom assessment, drawn from elementary, middle, and high school classrooms. We are well aware of the complex and time-consuming demands of teaching; practitioners need to find simple, immediately useful ways of assessing their students and determining the effectiveness of their instruction. We hope this book provides a sensible guide to achieving the objectives of efficiency and usefulness in assessment.

ASSESSMENT PRACTICES

The Charlotte-Mecklenburg School District in North Carolina joined eleven major city school systems that participated in an analysis of reading and math scores, using tests from the National Assessment of Educational Progress (NAEP). Charlotte's schools had the highest NAEP scores in all categories except eighth grade math, where it tied with Austin, Texas. When scores were broken out for Hispanic students, fourth graders in Charlotte and Austin tied for the highest scores in reading. In math, Charlotte's Hispanic students were ranked number one. Charlotte's teachers give much of the credit for their district's fine record, especially with disadvantaged students, to assessment and prompt follow-up (Tomsho, 2005).

The district uses a system of brief (thirty-item) tests designed by the school district's staff and administered quarterly during the school year. Teachers receive an analysis of their students' scores within a week, and low-performing students are immediately scheduled to meet with tutors and specialists. These tests are locally prepared, based on the district's curriculum objectives. With only thirty items, no one in the district would argue that these are perfect assessments, but they work; that is, they provide prompt and adequate indications of students' achievement, and of individuals' and classes' needs for specific instruction.

Note the characteristics of Charlotte's approach: The assessments are brief, administered quarterly, based on the actual curricula, and prepared by the school district's own teachers. The results are used to provide prompt feedback and remediation. It's also true that the district must commit resources to creating and grading the tests, and to remedying students' deficiencies that the tests reveal. We heartily endorse these assessment activities.

Another attempt to use frequent tests to diagnose and resolve learning problems was announced in 2007 by the chancellor of New York City's school system (Bosman, 2007, B1). We must await the implementation and results to judge the feasibility of New York's intended approach, but the complex assessment plan is interesting; if it proves workable it could provide practical guidance, especially for large school systems.

The New York plan has the city school system contracting with a mainline test publisher to prepare five tests a year in both reading and math for grades three through eight, and four tests per year in each subject for high school students. Tests in more subjects are to follow in subsequent years. The tests are designed to fit into a 45-minute class period and can be taken either online or by paper and pencil. Results of the online tests will be immediately available, scores from paper and pencil exams will become available within five days.

According to the chancellor, Joel Klein, "Teachers will be able to draw from a bank of questions to customize the tests to their own curriculum, choosing from a mix of multiple-choice or open-ended questions." It was not clear from the newspaper report how teachers would select the exam questions "from their own curriculum," how the test results would be evaluated, or how teachers will provide remedial help where it is needed. The sheer size of New York City's school population (1.1 million students) and the several innovative qualities of the testing program make this an important initiative to follow.

OUR READERS

Who should read this book to realize at least some of the benefits of assessment? Our primary audience is classroom teachers and administrators working in elementary, middle, or high schools. These are busy people, whose duties leave them little time for research; they must focus on dealing promptly and effectively with problems of classroom learning and assessment. We attempt to focus the principles and applications of assessment in light of the severe demands on teachers' and administrators' time.

We believe that prospective teachers and the faculty of schools of education may also find useful information about techniques for assessing and evaluating student achievement. There are texts that provide more complex and detailed information on assessment than we attempt here. Among these texts, we have found N. E. Gronlund's *Assessment of Student Achievement* (2006) especially useful in teaching our own education courses. This text is notable for its explanation of the nuances of multiple-choice item construction and of statistical procedures. Another publication by R. L. Stiggins, *Assessment for Student Learning* (2004), provides a wealth of valuable information on formative assessment in the classroom (assessment *for* learning, as the authors define it). Similarly, Sue Wortham's text, *Assessment in Early Childhood Education* (2005), is a fine presentation of the benefits and pitfalls in various approaches to assessing young children. We do not intend to replicate the detailed or targeted information in these excellent texts; rather we want to provide the reader with a basic, immediately useful understanding of the context and practices of good assessment in standard classrooms.

Further, we believe that several groups of educational shareholders would find much value in reviewing the benefits and costs of student assessment, and the appropriate and less appropriate uses of the results of student assessment. Many parents might welcome explanations of how their children's learning is assessed and how they can help their children do their best on classroom and standardized tests, what teachers' grades and scores on standardized test mean, and how much importance parents and students should attach to those scores and grades.

Other potential beneficiaries include school board members: When boards become conversant with the basics of assessment and evaluation, they can better monitor their schools' outcomes and formulate sensible expectations and policies. Another target audience is legislators who mandate statewide assessments for their schools and oversee the state departments commissioned to supervise that assessment. The intent of state testing legislation is excellent, but it is clear that some of these mandates and their implementation are not sufficiently founded on basic principles of measurement, such as validity, reliability, and efficiency, which we explain in chapter 2. We believe this book's contents could assist a variety of educational shareholders in discussing and formulating education policy.

OUR FOCUS

Many student characteristics can be assessed: academic success, athletic prowess, social skills, and so on. We are concentrating in this volume on *academic achievement*. In several chapters, we will refer to the importance of social and emotional growth for students, but we treat these topics in the context of students successfully mastering the basics of academic disciplines in their elementary school grades, then extending their interests and exploring subjects more in depth during their middle and high school years. Our reasons for this academic focus are as follows:

- Facilitating academic achievement is something that schools can and should do; it is their basic function and should be their primary goal. If schools fail in this task, it is unlikely that other institutions of society will compensate for the failure. This obligation for academic achievement is not confined to teaching the basics of reading, writing, and arithmetic, but includes science, social studies, languages and literature, the arts, and physical education.
- Social and emotional goals like fostering self-esteem are very important for children to achieve, so it is appropriate for schools to further them, as well. But the primary goal of schools, the purpose that schools are best equipped to achieve, is academic achievement. Note that academic success can contribute markedly to social and emotional gains for students.
- As students move through high school and into college, their ability to learn more demanding subjects will depend heavily on their "literacy" within content areas. This includes the abilities to read and understand complex texts, to write clearly and creatively, and to have a solid foundation for the demands of higher mathematics. The importance of these skills accounts for their emphasis in assessment at the K–12 levels.

So, our text focuses on the assessment of academic learning, beginning with measuring students' success in reading, writing, and mathematics in elementary school, then expanding to other subjects in middle and high school.

If schools concentrate on fundamental academic learning, can they preserve other important elements in the curriculum? Recently, a newspaper headline read, "Schools cut back subjects to push reading and math." In the third paragraph, the writer states, "The changes appear to principally affect schools and students who test below grade level" (Dillon, 2006, A1). In most schools today, in the primary and middle school grades, students who are deficient in reading and/or math are being required to spend more time on those subjects. The article quotes several educators who lament the loss of school time for history, science, and the arts, as well as recess periods. These subjects, as well as occasional times to allow children to run around, talk, and recharge their batteries, are indeed essential components of good schooling.

We believe that students in desperate need of basic remediation in language and math skills require intensive tutoring, longer school days, and more days of school during the year. They can also advance more rapidly with a structured approach to teaching. These strategies have proven successful in some schools whose students are seriously deficient in basic learning. Several of these success stories are described in chapter 1.

Researchers have focused on various qualities that contribute to positive outcomes in virtually all elements of students' lives (Duckworth and Seligman, 2005). The qualities include perseverance, patience, organization, and time management, as well as the ability to work productively in groups with other students. These characteristics are credited with having more influence on success, whether in school or throughout adult life, than an intensive focus on academic achievement. Thus, the argument is made that schools should spend less time teaching and assessing academic achievement, and concentrate more on inculcating these "character habits." Other research also points to good work habits, that is, those related to regular and focused study as being vital to success in school and thereafter.

We generally concur with this research. However, it doesn't follow that teachers should concentrate on teaching good study habits *at the expense of* course knowledge and skills. Placing academic achievement in artificial opposition to good character traits and work habits can lead to classroom games and exercises, group projects, and unfocused discussions that have little to do with learning the knowledge and skills taught in courses; such activities ill-prepare students to use their learning in increasingly complex ways. We believe it is in the context of academic learning that teachers should inculcate good work habits. Again, we choose to focus on the link between assessment and academic achievement, not at the expense of work habits, study skills, and emotional well-being, but rather as a focusing lens with which to view these areas.

AN OUTLINE

The table of contents provides an overview of our text, but a few explanatory comments may be helpful. In part I, we establish a context for student assessment. The first chapter speaks to the background for assessment.

While our focus is on what teachers can apply in their classrooms, we feel it's important at the beginning of our text to consider the reasons for the enormous differences in assessment results for students in the poorest inner-city and rural areas, in contrast with the results in more affluent suburban school systems. That background chapter includes a discussion of how student assessment is entwined with social class and with national, state, and local politics, as well as the impact of state and federal testing mandates on teachers and administrators. Chapter 2 addresses the fundamentals of assessment: what assessment is and is not, and what it can and cannot do.

Part II ushers in the "how to do it" of classroom assessment. Chapter 3 addresses the three principal reasons teachers assess their students. Chapters 4 through 6 cover techniques of classroom testing, from multiple-choice and matching items to fill-in items, essays, performance assessments, and observations. We explain when each technique is most effective and how to prepare and score them efficiently.

Part III covers standardized measurements: because teachers and administrators are usually responsible for administering standardized tests and interpreting the scores, we devote chapters 7 and 8 to defining their purposes, limitations, and appropriate uses of results. In chapters 9 and 10, we present recommendations for preparing students for assessment and compare the advantages and limitations of standardized tests with those devised by classroom teachers.

Part IV deals with grading and reporting the results of student assessment. Chapter 11 explains summative progress reports, that is, the use of assessment results for making decisions about students, teachers, and schools. Chapter 12 is a "how to do it" chapter on reporting results of assessment to students, parents, and other interested parties.

Part V consolidates and extends what has gone before by addressing the larger issues of program evaluation and accountability. In chapter 13, we point out the need for teachers and administrators to assess and evaluate all elements of their curriculum, and we suggest several approaches with varying degrees of rigor in conducting those evaluations. The final chapter on accountability attempts to delineate the responsibilities of all participants in school teaching and learning, including students and parents, as well as school professionals. In this chapter, we again discuss the complexities of using student test scores to evaluate teachers' performance.

We conclude by providing a glossary of measurement terms, a references and bibliography section, and two appendixes. The first appendix is an example of one school's total plan for assessment; the second suggests content and strategies for an in-service workshop on student assessment.

Throughout the book, we often use the terms "test" and "assessment" interchangeably. Strictly, "assessment" refers not only to the gathering of data but suggests some appraisal of its meaning. Standardized tests could be termed *assessments*, as they usually include some interpretative information, but everyone refers to them simply as "tests." When we speak of "evaluation," we mean the process of drawing inferences, reaching conclusions, and making decisions from the data generated by assessment. Periodic reports sent to parents on their children's progress are an example of evaluation, that is, they summarize teachers' judgments that are based on multiple assessments of students' achievement.

THE AUTHORS

The two authors differ in generation, training, and experience, so it's no surprise that while agreeing on most theories and practices in schooling we disagree about some of them. One of us, Jim, is primarily oriented toward the needs of in-service teachers and administrators, while Chris tends to think first about preparing pre-service and assisting beginning teachers. We'll try to indicate where we see issues differently from one another, and to articulate views that give fair exposure to those who disagree with one or both of us. This attempt at evenhandedness will not earn the approval of those who passionately espouse either a "radical" or a "reactionary" approach to schooling. Certainly, we will not satisfy the "all or nothing" reader who wants to rank, reward, retain, or fire teachers solely on the basis of their students' test scores, nor will we please those who believe that testing students and assigning grades is unethical and should be banned from the schools.

As we state earlier, our intent is to provide busy, hardworking teachers and administrators with a text on the context and efficient practices of good assessment. What we as authors and educators share with all readers, even the most extreme among them, is a desire to provide the best possible education to all our children. That commitment unites the authors with each other and with all who may disagree on means, but share the goal of helping students learn.

I

UNDERSTANDING ASSESSMENT

Chapter 1 discusses public education as a prelude to the chapters that follow; that background information addresses issues and practices in both classroom and standardized assessment.

The sheer size and complexity of public education in the United States makes generalizations about schools difficult and subject to contrary examples. We point out one generalization that is not, in itself, inaccurate but leads to false conclusions: on average, African Americans and Latinos score lower on standardized tests than their white or Asian counterparts.

A factor that certainly can influence student achievement is extreme poverty. But some schools have demonstrated an ability to teach impoverished students in ways that largely overcome the behavioral and cognitive disadvantages that frequently accompany extreme poverty. Clear policies for classroom behavior and appropriate modes of instruction are keys to learning; timely assessment and prompt use of results are keys to understanding and furthering students' academic achievement.

Several examples describe some schools' successes in teaching children who are not prepared to learn in a classroom. Commonly cited reasons for students' success or failure in school are evaluated.

Public education is and must be political, that is, the responsibility of officials at all levels of government. Educators' current focus of concern is the federal No Child Left Behind Act. The assessment provisions of the Act are listed, as are the problems and the effects of implementing the Act. We suggest that, without assessments common to all the states, the positive effects of NCLB will remain modest.

Chapter 2, The Basics of Assessment, describes the three essentials of good measurement: validity, reliability, and efficiency. We then explain a

1

few statistical terms that teachers encounter, especially as they interpret the results of standardized testing.

Next, we review the fundamental questions teachers must ask—and answer—as they plan their own assessments of their students. We close part I by clarifying the roles of the various parties in student assessment: the students and their parents, teachers, administrators, and school trustees.

1

Social and Political Realities of Assessment

Young low-income and minority children are more likely to start school without having gained important school readiness skills, such as recognizing letters and counting. . . . By the fourth grade, low-income students read about three grades behind non-poor students. Across the nation, only 15 percent of low-income fourth graders achieved proficiency in reading, compared with 41 percent of non-poor students.

—Center for American Progress and Institute for America's Future

The kids who need the most help—poor children from inner cities and rural areas—often attend the worst schools.

—R. Herbert

A CAUTIONARY NOTE

Before describing specifics of the social and political factors that affect schooling, we should mention several hazards in writing about our nation's schools. There are some 50 million children attending public schools in this country; they are taught by 3.2 million teachers in some 15,000 school districts. These numbers should immediately make us wary of sweeping generalizations: For example, one hears the assertion, "Children from severely impoverished homes do poorly in school." Yes, children in most families that live in extreme poverty lag in academic achievement. But that deficit is not true for all disadvantaged children in every school, as some remarkably successful inner-city schools have demonstrated. In this book, we'll try to qualify broad assertions about American schools, teachers, and students. But readers must still be cautious when we make statements that, supposedly, are always and everywhere valid.

RACE, POVERTY, AND ACHIEVEMENT

Research has repeatedly demonstrated that student test scores correlate highly with parental income and with race; students from affluent white and Asian families tend to score higher than other racial and ethnic groups on standardized tests, like those used for college admissions. Another indicator of the relationship between family income, race, and school success is the high school dropout rate. Nationwide, about 72 percent of the girls in the high school class of 2003 graduated, while 65 percent of the boys earned diplomas. By far the highest percentage of dropouts is in the poorest inner-city and rural areas of the nation with heavy minority populations. Several researchers have described the negative impact of student mobility on student achievement; see Rumberger and Larson (1998) and Greene and Winters (2006).

Journalists and other commentators on test score discrepancies and dropout rates usually focus on racial differences, with African Americans, Latinos, and Native Americans heavily overrepresented on the negative end of both measures. We believe that the constant linking of low test scores and high dropout rates to race and ethnic origins leads to the common error of confusing correlation with causality. Students do not achieve or fail to achieve in school *because of* their racial or ethnic background. Rather, these students come from families that are greatly overrepresented in the ranks of the severely impoverished. The detrimental effects of extreme poverty on students' health, school attendance, readiness to learn, motivation, and behavior—all factors that bear on school achievement—are painfully obvious, especially in the poorest areas of our cities. Nevertheless, federal and state laws require reporting standardized test scores by race. We believe that this emphasis, however well intended, leads to erroneous stereotypical thinking. Because more Asian and white students score better on tests than do black, Latino, or Native American students, the knowledge and skills that underlie the scores tend to be attributed to socially intractable qualities, that is, race and ethnicity. In effect, we associate student success or failure with what students are, rather than with a possible contributory factor, such as their families' socioeconomic status, or with the most significant factor, how they are taught.

Another problem that derives from concentrating on test scores of racial groups is a temptation to believe that "they" just can't learn but it's not a problem for "my" racial or ethnic group. In fact, the shortfall in academic achievement is by no means restricted to one or a few racial groups. One study of two states (Rhode Island and Kentucky) shows that *40 percent* of the workforce in those states has difficulty performing basic skills like reading, writing, and simple arithmetic (Davies, 2006). Certainly, this deficit in basic skills is not confined to racial minorities.

Is poverty the common cause of low school achievement? The case is stronger here, but again, we are in danger of attributing causality to numbers; low academic achievement is more prevalent among poor children than among the affluent. If poverty were always and everywhere a cause of low academic achievement, children would never succeed academically unless they were taken out of poverty. Yet we know that some schools with populations of very poor children produce graduates with strong academic records and high rates of acceptance to colleges.

Clearly, severe poverty induces conditions or handicaps associated with sporadic school attendance and low academic achievement. Although schools cannot "cure" poverty, they can moderate some of the inhibitors to learning that often accompany poverty. For example, if a child comes to school without having eaten breakfast, a school can provide the nourishment he needs to function in class. A child with a vision or hearing problem that is not addressed in her home can be examined by a school nurse and referred to a physician or clinic. If there are no books or a place to study at home, a school can at least partly compensate for those deficiencies. Fortunately, schools are now required to provide a rough estimate of the number of their students who can be deemed "poor"; the metric commonly used is the percentage of students who receive free or reduced-fee school lunches. This measure at least suggests how many children are impoverished and where they are in school.

However, we contend that the basic cause of students' academic deficiencies documented by assessment is to be found in the schools, not in the students themselves or even primarily in the economic status of their families. The great majority of students who do not learn in school are not prepared to learn and are not being taught in appropriate ways. They are not subject to behavioral norms that are consistently enforced in the school and supported in the students' homes. In short, such students are not being instructed through methods and teaching strategies that can result in academic progress for the great majority of low-achieving students.

We are convinced of this explanation through our own study and experience of teaching and observing students, and especially by evaluations from an increasing number of schools that are successfully teaching students of every racial, ethnic, and economic background. The evidence for these successes is found in the results of student and program assessment, including standardized tests, teacher observation, measures of parental satisfaction, student reports, high school graduation rates, and college admissions data. Accordingly, a later section in this chapter is devoted to schools where assessment and evaluation have shown to be successful, and to an analysis of how and why they succeed.

Before we consider further this primary responsibility of schools for teaching and learning, we want to reflect more on the evidence that socio-economic status (SES), that is, affluence and poverty, correlates highly with school achievement. Why is that finding true, especially at the extremes of affluence and poverty?

Consider how the lives of children in the highest socioeconomic families typically differ from those in the lowest SES levels, and the impact of these conditions. We will arbitrarily refer to those families in the United States who are in the upper 20 percent of income as "affluent," and those in the lowest 20 percent as "poor." Those in the lowest 5 percent to 10 percent of income nationally may be considered in "severe" or "extreme poverty."

THE INFLUENCE OF AFFLUENCE AND POVERTY

Conditions related to affluence that affect schooling include the following:

- Affluent families live in communities and school districts with strong financial and moral support for their local schools. That support translates into resources, both human and material, for their schools (Greene and Winters, 2006).
- As schools in these fortunate communities attract children from high SES families, expectations for student achievement increase. These affluent parents make clear their anticipation that their children will succeed in school and will go on to college and graduate or professional education.
- The homes of children from affluent families can provide facilities and schedule time for children to read, study, and compute.
- Their neighborhoods are safe, and their friends and families who live around them prize education and encourage academic achievement.
- Levels of parental education correlate strongly with affluence. The better educated parents are in a community, the more likely it is that the community will have significant human and monetary resources and will be willing to devote these resources to the schools.
- Such parents are comfortable interacting with their children's teachers and administrators, and tend to be outspoken about their expectations that their children's schools show excellent results on measures of school quality like college admissions or state assessments.

The sociologist Annette Lareau believes that affluent parents engage in what she calls "concerted cultivation," through heavy oversight of their children's homework and school achievement, and weekends and vacations crammed with organized enrichment activities (Lindsey, 2007). To some educators and parents, this focus appears overdone and stressful for both children and parents. But it's also true that this intense concentration inculcates the intellectual, organizational, and social skills that are rewarded in today's economy.

Conditions associated with extreme poverty that impact learning include:

- Physical health: most very poor families have inadequate access to medical care and insufficient money and/or time to prepare regular, nutritious meals for their children.
- Impoverished inner-city families tend to move frequently and some may be essentially homeless.
- Children in these families suffer sleep deprivation and disorientation; they are frequently absent from school.
- Cognitive development: young children acquire language skills (the keystone of school achievement) by all kinds of verbal interactions with adults and other children. When speaking and listening are not extensively practiced in a home, when no one reads to children or encourages them to read, they come to school less ready to learn than their more fortunate peers. These children often lack access to general information that school subjects build upon. This information deficit may be in facts about themselves, their communities, and the history of their own or other countries. Or they may simply be unfamiliar with the basic vocabulary that texts and teachers use in class. One educator refers to this basic information as "enabling knowledge."
- Deficits in social development will inhibit a child's learning in a school that does not recognize and compensate for those deficits. Some behaviors that children in our poorest neighborhoods learn as survival skills prove dysfunctional in a typical school environment.
- Finally, most of the advantages of affluent families and well-educated parents mentioned previously are absent in impoverished families. Very poor parents tend to be among the least educated members of our society; many are recent immigrants, with modest English language skills. Those who are reasonably healthy often must work several jobs to provide basic necessities for their families. The neighborhoods in which they can find housing may be dangerous and chaotic. Most significant, the great majority of children from these families must attend schools that do not provide them with resources they need, plus a set of rules and a program of instruction that provide the basics required for academic achievement.

What is the relationship between affluence, poverty, and school achievement? It is easy to show a strong relationship between poverty and low achievement in schools, when these schools do not adjust teaching to the needs their students bring with them. It's also correct to say that, on average, students from affluent homes score well on standardized tests and other measures of academic achievement. Whether the more fortunate students' successes are attributable to a good "fit" with their schools' curricula, or to the training and motivation they receive in their homes and communities, is difficult to disentangle. When, for example, affluent suburban high schools offer a large array of Advanced Placement courses and encourage students to enroll and succeed in them, they are certainly providing a curriculum that meets many of their students' needs and interests.

However, it is equally true that when inner-city schools provide conditions and curricula that respond to their students needs, these schools consistently attain high student achievement in state examinations, high graduation rates, and a high percentage of graduates who go on to college. These are the results obtained in the Knowledge Is Power Programs, North Star Academy, and other successful schools described later in this chapter.

The bottom line for student learning is not that affluence equals success, while poverty means failure; rather, that all schools should be required to and be given assistance to adjust their curricula to meet the needs that students bring to school. Strategies that work in the suburbs are frequently unsuccessful in the inner cities or poorest rural areas of our country, and vice versa. But what do the preceding statements about school curriculum and environment have to do with the subject of this text—student assessment— that is, the systematic gathering of data on students' academic achievement? Consider these questions:

- How can we demonstrate that students in some schools are making far greater academic progress than their counterparts in other schools? By assessing all students with valid and reliable instruments, and then comparing results by schools and subgroups.
- How do we know what school subjects and elements within the subjects are learned well or poorly? By analyzing assessment results.
- How do we know when a student or group of students is falling behind in learning? By evaluating the results of assessment, including teachers' observations.
- How do we know that some teaching strategies induce satisfactory learning results in certain students and not in others? By teaching, that is, applying the strategies, then assessing the results.

Appropriate teaching is the key to learning; assessment is the key to learning whether teaching is appropriate and successful.

EDUCATIONAL RESOURCES AND STUDENT ACHIEVEMENT

If assessment shows the disparity in outcomes between students from affluent families and those from very poor homes, can we assume that the monetary resources devoted to poor urban or rural schools differ greatly from those spent on wealthier districts? Yes and no. In 2007, the national average expenditure per pupil was $8,700, up 3 percent from the previous year. But the amount of tax funds committed to school districts differs greatly by state and community.

In New Jersey, poor urban areas like Newark and Jersey City receive as much as, and sometimes considerably more than, the state average of $13,800 per student—second highest in the country. In Massachusetts, Minnesota, and twenty-one other states, more tax dollars are provided to economically depressed areas than to average or affluent districts (Education Commission of the States, 2004). This funding usually comes through supplements from the state to districts with low property tax bases. On the other end of the scale, Utah expends $5,257 per student, and Arizona, $6,281. In low-funding states like Utah and Arizona, the poorest school districts may be at the bottom of the state's range of funding. Given that the needs of children in the depressed areas of these low-support states are greater than those in more affluent areas, we could conclude that low test scores and other indicators of nonachievement may be due, at least in part and in some districts, to inadequate resources.

That said, in Newark, which is New Jersey's largest school district with some 43,000 students, the per-student budget of more than $18,000 exceeds the New Jersey average expenditure by more than $4,000. This is a sum educators in most states would be delighted to receive and would consider more than adequate to provide a sound education for all students. If students in Newark schools were showing strong results on measures of learning, the extra investment in that district would appear well merited. But Newark's public schools have the high dropout rates, low test scores, and small number of students continuing their education in college that characterize most large-city school systems. Ironically, the head of the Newark Teachers' Union complains of academically successful charter schools draining off funds from the Newark system, although the average per pupil cost in Newark's charter schools is $10,000.

There are a few hopeful signs in Newark. A vigorous new mayor has targeted that city's schools as a priority for reform. New Jersey's Department of Education recommended in July 2007 that the Newark school system be "partially removed" from the list of schools in New Jersey that were taken away from local board control and placed under the direct supervision of the state. The positive recommendation is based on some evidence of better management in the district.

No one would argue that Newark's teachers have an easy task. But if the system would implement the disciplinary policies, the focus on parental cooperation, and the academic expectations and curriculum that prevail in Newark's high achieving charter schools, students and teachers in the Newark system would experience more success.

We have noted that New Jersey is one of the states that provide substantial supplementary funding for poverty-area school systems; this funding is in response to lawsuits engendered by the deficits in achievements noted in the state's urban schools. Unfortunately, this reform concentrated on increasing revenue to these urban schools, without putting in place requirements for measurable improvement in student achievement. The high level of funding and low level of achievement of public schools in Newark and other large urban centers in New Jersey indicate that the state has not yet identified all the means necessary to achieve its educational ends.

WHY DO SOME INNER-CITY SCHOOLS SUCCEED?

In trying to understand the failure of even well-funded inner-city schools, it may be helpful to compare them with schools that offer alternatives within impoverished urban school districts.

The Broad Foundation is dedicated to improving student achievement in America's lowest-performing schools. The Foundation annually gives a large cash award to an urban, high-poverty public school district that shows substantial progress in raising student achievement. In 2007, the five districts named as finalists for the awards were Bridgeport, Connecticut, Public Schools; Long Beach, California, Unified School District; Miami-Dade County, Florida, Public Schools; New York City Department of Education; and Northside Independent School District in San Antonio, Texas (Broad Foundation, 2007). In October 2007, New York City's schools received the Broad prize. The school system was cited "for having made the greatest improvement in student achievement, particularly in closing the gap between white and minority students" (Medina, 2007).

Schools and school systems like those recognized by the Broad Foundation have certain commonalities: they identify students in need of special help as early as possible, they provide tutoring and other support, and they have restructured their curricula to ensure a concentration and continuity in developing basic skills, notably in language arts and math. Especially in the elementary grades, these schools commonly use teaching methods radically different and more intensive than those in more traditional schools. They usually have longer days and more instructional hours per day. They set specific, measurable interim and final learning goals, and frequently assess their achievement. These successful schools also teach values and require conformity to a code of classroom behavior.

The Education Trust conducts research on improving high schools with large populations of students who are struggling academically. We commend the Trust's report, *Gaining Traction, Gaining Ground* (Education Trust, 2005). The report describes practices in "high impact" schools that appear to result in substantial gains in student achievement. Among the many significant findings that refer to school culture, teachers and administrators' practices, and curriculum, we note these successful schools' use of assessment data for *planning* for student resources and curriculum changes, not simply for reviewing past student performance.

We should add that these outstanding schools have administrators and teachers who are willing to go the extra mile for their students. An example of such a teacher is Rafe Esquith, who tells of teaching in a Los Angeles school situated in an area rife with poverty and violence (Esquith, 2007). A majority of Esquith's fifth graders struggle with English as their second language, but they show dramatic results on California's language arts exams. These students exemplify a point we make repeatedly in this book: the critical importance of students' and parents' own efforts in response to dedicated teaching. Many of Esquith's fifth graders come to school voluntarily at 6:30 a.m. for "pre-school" instruction. They remain at school until 5:00 p.m., and those who can, come for more instruction during vacations.

North Star Academy

Some notable successes in improving inner-city education have been achieved by parochial and public charter schools. These schools draw on essentially the same population as the local public system, and they operate on budgets that range from lower than the regular system for charter schools, to much, much lower for parochial schools. North Star Academy Charter School in Newark, New Jersey, enrolls students in middle and high school (North Star Academy Charter School, 1997–2006). It is a good example of a school that succeeds under the same handicaps that afflict failing schools in the Newark School District. (Ninety percent of North Star's students qualify for free or reduced-fee lunch.) Over its ten years in existence, North Star has developed several assessment indicators on which to judge the school's success (U.S. Department of Education Office of Innovation and Improvement, 2006):

- High school graduation rates: In 2005, all twelfth grade regular education students graduated.
- College placement: For the graduating classes of 2004, 2005, and 2006, North Star placed 95 percent of its graduates in four-year colleges, the

highest ranking among all high schools in New Jersey. In 2007, 100 percent of North Star's graduates were admitted to college, 95 percent to four-year colleges.

- State test results for high school: On the High School Proficiency Assessment, every North Star eleventh grader scored proficient or above in language arts, and 92.3 percent scored proficient or above in math (J. Verrilli, principal; conversation, August 15, 2007).
- State test results for middle school: In the eighth grade, 93.5 percent of students were proficient in language arts, 77 percent were proficient in math, and 88 percent were proficient in science. These results are double the comparable Newark system schools and well above the state average. Of course, as a public school, North Star cannot pick and choose its students.

Several statistics for North Star are especially meaningful when they are compared with one another: first, the poverty level: 90 percent of the school's students are on the free or reduced-fee lunch plan; second, the 100 percent graduation rate and college enrollment; third, the per-student cost of $9,090 per year.

Why do a majority of students in schools like North Star stay in school, score well on state tests, and go on to college? The school has created a culture of academic success and reinforces it with teachers, parents, and, frequently, students during the school day. The school requires assessments every eight weeks in all classes. Results of the assessments are reviewed by teachers, department chairs, and administrators. Teachers respond to evidence of deficiencies among groups of students by re-teaching the topic, and using different teaching strategies. Individual students who are falling behind immediately begin tutoring sessions, with extra help available on Saturday mornings. Like many other successful inner-city schools, North Star has an extended school year.

During the school year, parent involvement and cooperation is furthered by frequent calls from North Star teachers and by asking parents to come to the school to pick up their children's report cards. Conferences with teachers are scheduled during those visits. One indicator of parental attitudes: some 1,600 students are on the school's waiting list.

We see two prerequisites as critical for this and similar schools' success: First, the trustees, administrators, and faculty in these schools adjust their curricula and student management procedures (also known as discipline) to fit the needs of their student population. These adjustments are easier for charter and most parochial schools because their administrators and boards are specific to their schools; they are not part of a larger, sometimes much larger, school system. Second, these successful schools strongly encourage parents to pledge their support of the schools' policies on discipline and to monitor their children's attendance, home-work, and grades.

Note that classroom discipline figures prominently in both explanations just cited. Chris Deneen has, for several years, mentored teachers in New York City's public schools. He has observed some classrooms in which student learning is clearly taking place. But in other schools, chaos reigns in the classrooms. Students ignore the teacher, sleep, talk, and wander in and out of class. The victims of this behavior are the students who want to learn and, in a real sense, their teachers, who are driven out of their minds and/or out of teaching by classrooms in which teaching and learning cannot take place.

Charter Schools

In citing examples from successful charter schools, we intend to endorse success, not charter schools. A 2006 report from the National Center for Education Statistics, using data from 2003, found that students in traditional public school fourth grades had higher National Assessment of Educational Progress (NAEP) scores than students in the charter schools sample (Schemo, 2006). However, that report suffers from a problem that raises questions about the conclusions drawn from the study: it measures status, not progress; that is, it gives us no clear information about the contribution of the schools to children's progress in reading and math. Certainly, we want to know where students stand in achievement, but to judge a school's effects, we have to know where its students started and how far they have come. The study compares 376,000 students in nearly 6,800 traditional public elementary schools with 6,500 students in 150 charter schools. Necessarily, such a large-scale study speaks to averages within enormous ranges; some schools in each group are achieving outstanding results and others are performing poorly.

We are interested in examining what successful schools, especially those in our poorest school districts, are doing that seems to contribute to their success. We use some examples from charter schools because these schools are obliged by state laws and public opinion to account annually for their results; some charter schools have been forced to close when they have not achieved expected results over just a few years' existence. Under the No Child Left Behind Act, that threat now applies to all public schools. But variations in state standards and protracted schedules for reform make penalties less probable or severe than for charter schools. Because they compete with traditional schools for students, charter schools must be able to show "value added" by means of a variety of assessments; these may be quantitative, for example, test scores or college admissions, and/or qualitative measures like parental satisfaction or students' attitudes toward learning.

Parochial schools differ from their public counterparts in that they are free to make student behavior a criterion for remaining in a school. In public schools, statutes for suspension and expulsion of students vary by state, but state regulations tend to constrain such penalties with the laudable intent of protecting the rights of offending students and their parents. In states with strict oversight of charter schools, rules for enforcing discipline by suspension or expulsion are usually the same as for the "regular" school systems.

However, it should be noted that many of those on the firing line—teachers and administrators—feel that the rules often protect the rights of disruptive students at the expense of the rights of other children to orderly classrooms in which they can learn. Teachers complain of one or a few chronically unruly students whom they are unable to have removed from the classrooms. These teachers do not advocate throwing the offending students out on the streets, but they are aware that such students need a different learning environment than the usual classroom can provide. We are highly sympathetic to these teachers' concerns; it should, however, be noted that some alternative public schools that enroll all applicants and are equally subject to state regulations are frequently successful in maintaining orderly classrooms. Why the disparity in student behavior?

A significant advantage public charter schools and their parochial counterparts enjoy is that students are not assigned to them: parents choose to enroll their children. (This is true in a few public systems as well.) These parents have a natural desire to validate their choice by encouraging their children to follow school rules and to study and achieve. In these parental attitudes we see the second condition for success: cooperation between school and home. Prior to the enrollment of students, many charter and parochial schools request that parents come to the school for an explanation of the school's expectations for student behavior; parents are urged to promise their support for school rules, sometimes in a written "contract." Parents further pledge to respond promptly and cooperatively to calls or notes from the school concerning their children's behavior or academic deficiencies.

Students in these schools are presented with the school's code of behavior and are frequently reminded of the benefits of adhering to it as well as the penalties for violating it. Teachers and administrators agree on what is good, or tolerable, or unacceptable behavior; teachers apply the rewards and penalties consistently, and they are supported in their decisions by their administrators. No one should be surprised that these procedures are not followed perfectly, nor do they work all the time. All schools are staffed by fallible human beings. Practices like those we describe simply work better and more often than others.

In these educationally disadvantaged but successful classrooms, a fast-paced, structured curriculum helps to hold students' attention; they are less likely to "drop out" mentally or cause distractions. This combination of clear and fairly enforced codes of behavior, parental cooperation, and fast-moving lesson plans—with constant student–teacher interactions to assess what has been learned and what needs to be re-taught—seems to be the key element in those alternative public schools that are successful.

Saying that such schools are successful is not to say they succeed "every day, in every way, with every child"—but orderly behavior and concentrated teaching bring far better results than disorder and unfocused instruction.

Successful Teaching

Principals are key figures in creating and maintaining such an orderly atmosphere. Teachers want to teach, and they want their students to learn. If codes of conduct are implemented in the classrooms, firmly upheld by school administrators, and supported by parents, teachers' lives will improve, as will those of their students.

Some teachers are not receptive to highly structured, teacher-directed lessons, arguing that these plans result in a loss of creativity on the part of both students and teachers. But human beings do not create something out of nothing. If students are to learn, they need a fund of information they can draw on; learning depends on prior learning (Hirsch, 1987).

It is true that highly structured lesson plans do not permit teachers to introduce many of their own ideas about how and when certain information and skills should be taught. The structured curriculum is intended to provide basic learning to students who lack it and who, if they do not grasp these fundamentals in elementary school, will not succeed in later grades. It is designed as well to mitigate the disciplinary problems that less-structured classrooms commonly experience. It's also true that highly structured instruction places the classroom teacher in the dominant role. She decides what will be studied, how, and for how long; she also promptly assesses her students' grasp of the topics.

For example, in teaching reading with one such approach, called "direct teaching," a teacher has students listen to a new word, repeat it aloud, see how it is spelled, then write it. When students understand the meaning and how to pronounce and spell new words, they are then encouraged to use this knowledge in creating new phrases and sentences of their own. So application and discovery follow direct teaching (Henderson, 2006). This approach originated with Carl Bereiter and Siegfried Englemann (1966). Direct teaching is not ideal for every classroom, and may not work at all with older and more advanced students who can draw on a broad base of learning and whose classroom behavior allows further learning to take place, but this structured approach or one like it is almost indispensable for students who lack that cumulative background.

A methodology sometimes encouraged in schools of education is small group discussions that are intended to help students internalize learning by interactions with their peers. There is much to be said for this approach in higher education, where students have something to contribute to each other, plus the basic self-discipline to conduct useful discussions. In urban schools with seriously disadvantaged populations, small group discussions usually result in little learning and lots of chaos.

Our views expressed here are not meant as endorsements of all alternative public schools or parochial schools. In terms of student achievement, some of them are better and some are worse than schools in public systems. Nor can results in all charter schools be compared with those in the public systems without considering the number of instructional hours in each system. In the Knowledge Is Power Program (KIPP) charter schools, for example, the school day is often 7:30 a.m. to 5:00 p.m., with four hours of Saturday instruction and an additional month in the summer. Admittedly, matching such a schedule would pose many problems for a typical inner-city school system. But KIPP schools are generally successful in areas that most inner-city schools are not; their students learn, graduate, and enroll in college. School boards and taxpayers cannot be immune to the principle, "Who wills the end, wills the means."

In the controversy over charter schools, partisans should concentrate, not on governance, but on the evidence of student learning; those results should be drawn from a variety of assessment measures. Educators should be asking how successful strategies can be imitated in schools with comparable populations.

Nor should educators ignore the message of the widespread acceptance of alternative schools by parents, especially those in urban school districts. Many state legislatures have imposed caps on the number of charters in their states and have refused to extend tax support to constructing school facilities, thus severely limiting the number of charter schools. It's clear that, without these restrictions, more students and parents would choose alternative public schools without having to languish on long waiting lists.

Furthermore, it is unfair to say that charter schools owe their success, where they are successful, to their freedom from state regulations. While 68 percent of the states have capped the number of charters they will grant, 95 percent require annual reports from charter schools, and all states hold charter schools to the rules for state standards and assessments (Hess and Petrilli, 2006).

WHY DO SOME INNER-CITY SCHOOLS FAIL?

We believe the following reasons explain the great majority of failures in inner-city schools:

- The primary reason for the failure of schools whose students bring with them the behavioral and learning handicaps that characterize severe poverty is the failure to adjust disciplinary rules and the curriculum to meet these students' needs. As indicated in a previous section (Why Do Some Inner-City Schools Succeed?), learning requires a commitment from both parents and students to a code of behavior, high expectations, and a program of fast-paced, demanding studies.
- The most difficult schools in which to teach are disproportionately staffed by inexperienced teachers. This practice, commonly mandated by union contracts, means that the most complex and demanding teaching is required of the least skilled teachers. It's pointless to blame the teachers' unions for protecting the interests of their members, and it's understandable that experienced teachers prefer the usually more orderly and familiar environment of middle-class schools. But frequently, the results of placing inexperienced teachers in inner-city classrooms are frustration for students, parents, and especially, for teachers, many of whom leave teaching after a few years of disappointing experiences.
- Recent graduates of teacher education programs have usually been taught subject content and teaching strategies suited (more or less) to students from middle-class families. It's understandable that these new teachers struggle when they try to teach a curriculum that is inappropriate for inner-city schools. As every principal knows, without skilled monitoring and support, first-year teachers usually struggle in whatever classroom they are assigned. Even the occasional teacher who is experienced in suburban schools and who moves to inner-city classrooms does not find the transition an easy one. But these teachers' experience has given them a repertoire of knowledge and skills plus the confidence that make possible their adjustment to new teaching conditions.
- The great majority of urban teachers and administrators are drawn from social environments with very different values from those of our most impoverished inner-city areas. Deferring to verbal direction, listening to adults, following rules, avoiding physical or verbal abuse of teachers and other students and respecting others' property are all rules that most teachers learned in their families and schools. Of course, these virtues are not practiced perfectly in any student population. Furthermore, students in high-poverty neighborhoods can find that breaking these rules is necessary for survival.
- As we've noted, some teachers complain that the imposition of state standards and assessments hinder teachers' creativity and professionalism by reducing teaching to prescribed, detailed lesson plans and considerable rote drill. This objection arises in part from social class differences in various schools; it's easy and enjoyable to be creative

with students who are reasonably well behaved and who receive a great
deal of their educational conditioning from their homes.

However, this complaint also reflects a generational difference. Most educated adults prefer to learn "creatively," that is, by developing their knowledge and understanding through reading and reflection, then through listening to and having exchanges with experts and with their peers. Variations of this creative approach can succeed in those middle schools and high schools in which students have mastered the two prerequisites for such instruction: self-discipline and the fundamental knowledge and learning skills that allow them to expand on or construct their own learning.

To encourage teachers to rely on these creative teaching strategies in most inner-city schools is like telling someone to build a house without a foundation, or without the tools of carpenters, plumbers, electricians, and so on. Good practitioners in every profession—medicine, counseling, teaching— employ the means that seem most likely to yield the results they seek. As teachers, they have a repertoire of skills, including an ability to assess and address the learning readiness and base of information their students need. They adapt their teaching to their clients' needs, rather than insisting that one approach fits all.

This background discussion of successful and unsuccessful schools may appear to omit a number of factors that contribute to teaching and learning problems in schools. Although this text is primarily devoted to issues of assessment, we will add a few more observations about frequently cited conditions in schools that contribute to success or failure, as demonstrated by assessments, in teaching and learning in schools.

  1. *A lack of adequate resources* is probably the most often cited cause for
     school failure. The deficiency may be extreme poverty on the part of
     the schools' pupils and/or an insufficiency of human and material re-
     sources in the school.

     We discuss this rationale in the sections on family poverty immedi-
     ately preceding and in the section on political realities that follows. All
     that government and private agencies can do will not eliminate
     poverty, although their efforts should aim to alleviate the effects of
     poverty on families, and especially on children, as much as possible.

     Nevertheless, the relationship between levels of school funding and
     students' academic success is weak. That statement may appear coun-
     terintuitive, but when schools in affluent suburbs succeed, it is not
     clear the extent to which their success is owed to factors other than
     funding. (See earlier section, The Influence of Affluence and Poverty.)
     When struggling inner-city schools are amply funded, they can fail to
     show improved student achievement. Conversely, when some urban
     and suburban public schools are funded at levels below those of their

neighboring schools, they succeed. They don't succeed because they are less well funded, but because they accommodate their instruction to the needs of their student bodies.

2. A good argument can be made for the *quality of staff* contributing to successful schools. The leadership of local administrators and the training and dedication of teachers are crucial elements in schools. We speak elsewhere in this book of the importance of teachers using instructional and assessment strategies that are proven to work with the students in their classrooms. But teachers can only be successful with the support of their principals and other supervisors. These administrators can provide in-service training, coaching, encouragement, and occasionally, defense from unreasonable criticism that teachers have a right to expect. With that support and guidance, even beginning teachers can often be successful by using appropriate teaching strategies in inner-city schools, as a number of urban schools have demonstrated.

3. *Class size*: It is an article of faith, especially among parents, that "small" classes enhance their children's learning. In fact, it is impossible to generalize about the impact of the teacher–student ratio on learning because results depend on so many other variables: the actual size of "small" and "large" classes, the subject being taught, the specific skills and knowledge being learned, the teaching strategies and techniques employed, the readiness of the students to learn, and the knowledge and skills of the teacher. A serious study that attempted to consider at least some of these elements is Project STAR, which concluded that smaller class sizes positively influenced reading and math scores in primary grade students. For an extensive discussion of this important issue, see *The Class Size Debate* (Krueger et al., 2002). But the number of factors affecting student achievement—above all, the quality of the teaching—makes generalizations difficult.

   Good teachers, using appropriate methods, can successfully teach certain skills to a class of thirty or more students. Unskilled teachers can fail with half that number. That said, administrators and trustees should still pay respectful attention to the strong preference of both parents and teachers for reducing class size. And it is true that in small classes, more attention can be paid to individual students and teachers have more time to grade tests, review homework, and comment on students' writing. If all things were equal, smaller classes would be more desirable than large ones but, practically, smaller classes mean more teachers and classrooms; unfortunately, the costs of smaller versus larger classes are not equal.

4. One significant reason why students fall behind in school is *mobility*. Every year in the United States, about 30 percent of children change schools; some change several times in a school year. According to one

Figure 1.1.   Two Essential Qualities of Successful Schools

Quality	Characteristics
Order	Rules for student behavior and study
	Commitment by parents to support rules
	Commitment by faculty to enforce rules
Instruction	High, measurable goals for learning
	Logical and sequential lesson plans
	Teaching for disadvantaged students that is intensive and directive
	Frequent assessment, prompt remediation

report (U.S. General Accounting Office, 1994), one in six U.S. third graders changed schools at least three times since beginning first grade. That astonishing percentage is surely even higher among children of migrant workers and in the poorest neighborhoods of our urban areas. In the process of moving, children may miss days or weeks of school. They are then placed in a new environment, with teachers and peers who are strangers to them. Because U.S. schools do not have common curricula, new students may take up their study of math or history at a point far ahead of or far behind that of their former school.

We summarize this discussion on why schools succeed and their essential qualities in figure 1.1.

We have spoken of other qualities of successful schools, for example, dedicated teachers and administrators, a lengthened school day and year, provisions for students with medical needs, a place to study, and so on. But we believe that, if school boards and administrators begin with the two essential qualities in figure 1.1, other important qualities of a successful school will begin to fall in place.

PUBLIC EDUCATION MUST BE POLITICAL

It's pointless to condemn the "intrusion of politics into public education." Public education is created by and subject to the control of the states; that authority is exercised through elected legislatures and school boards, and the state and local administrators they appoint. Public education is, inevitably and properly, political, in the sense that it is the business of the public and its representatives to regulate state and local school systems.

As a digression, we note that in times not long past, teaching and administrative positions were sometimes dispensed to those applicants who met decidedly unprofessional standards, like being related to a local political mogul or by bribing school board members.

In some large-city school districts, these abuses led to the formation of independent boards that became responsible for hiring teachers. These bodies, called boards of examiners, selected teachers and administrators in large part based on the scores they achieved on board-designed tests. Many states now require passing scores in standardized exams for teacher certification, and some local boards are rewarding teachers for passing stringent new assessments for advanced certification. Are we seeing, is this use of tests for teachers, déjà vu all over again?

STATE AND FEDERAL MANDATES

Today, educators complain not so much about corruption, but about state and federal mandates that set standards for student achievement, prescribe tests to determine that achievement, and provide penalties for schools whose students don't meet minimal learning standards. At the state level, standards and assessments are not new; many states have long prescribed the academic content that public schools should teach, with varying degrees of specificity and enforcement. For years, many states have also prescribed tests to determine whether students have, in fact, learned what the standards prescribe.

In 2001, Congress passed the No Child Left Behind Act (NCLB). The bill was signed by President George W. Bush in 2002, and almost immediately, began to affect public schools in the United States. The NCLB did not set learning standards or curriculum, or prescribe specific tests to determine achievement; these tasks were left to the states. What made the NCLB notable and controversial is the demand that schools failing to meet state standards as measured by each state's test scores must undertake a program of improvement. If positive results didn't follow, a series of escalating penalties kicked in; they could culminate in the closing of a school (Peterson and Hess, 2006).

The NCLB is being reviewed by Congress as this book goes to print. The realignment of political power that began with the 2006 elections and the upcoming presidential election in 2008 are affecting efforts to bring forth a new bill that would satisfy a divided Congress and survive a possible presidential veto. It seems certain, however, that NCLB will not be renewed without substantial changes in its assessment provisions. Even conservative supporters of NCLB agree that some elements of the Act are unrealistic; those who have consistently opposed the Act want it abolished or radically changed.

Let's look at the characteristics of that act as it operates in early 2008 and note how it relates to the rights and the roles of the fifty states. The NCLB is about assessment, accountability, and school choice. It requires tests in grades three through eight, plus one high school assessment in reading and mathematics; testing of science begins in the school year 2007–2008.

In this text, we speak almost exclusively of the Act's provisions for assessment; NCLB also includes sections related to Title I schools, reading instruction, Advanced Placement classes and examinations, teacher qualifications, safe schools, and many other issues. The overall goal of the Act is to make every public school student "proficient" in reading and mathematics by the year 2014. A basic principle of NCLB is that the scores of subgroups of students—the poor, minorities, those with limited English proficiency—are to be broken out, that is, simply not assimilated into class-, school-, or districtwide averages for reporting purposes.

However, there are some problems and concerns with NCLB:

- The states are free of federal control in setting their learning standards, devising the assessments to determine each state's achievement, and setting norms, that is, what constitutes success or failure on the tests. Seemingly, states do not have options concerning the "penalty phase" of the NCLB. But, in fact, by the standards they devise and the achievement levels they set for satisfactory performance, state legislatures and departments of education largely control which of their schools will be deemed satisfactory.

- Legislation intended to affect almost 96,000 schools in 15,000 public school systems is sure to be flawed, at least initially. Shortly after the Act began to be implemented, the federal Department of Education started to modify certain of the assessment requirements originally mandated by the NCLB. For example, in November 2005, the department gave permission for up to ten states to develop an accountability system that considers "evidence of growth," or students' *progress* over time, not simply their status in relation to a prescribed grade level. That change promised to alleviate a source of legitimate criticism of the Act and to reduce the tension between federal and local educators.

- Perhaps the most common complaint of state officials about the NCLB is that it is inadequately funded. Critics of the Act claim that Congress has imposed large-scale testing and remediation mandates on the states without providing sufficient monies to implement them. Historically, most states had testing programs in place prior to the enactment of NCLB, so they were not starting from zero budgets. But it's true that the NCLB imposes yearly examinations in all grades, while some states have been testing less frequently and in fewer grades. The follow-up requirement for tutoring low-scoring students in schools with unsatisfactory results, for example, is also a costly provision of NCLB. In fact, Congress has provided substantial funding, if not as much as states want, to implement the NCLB at the state and local levels.

- Another major concern about NCLB derives from the Act's definition of "adequate yearly progress" and a "failing school." Educators have pointed to the relatively small numbers of students in subgroups whose low scores can trigger major penalties; these decisions are questionable on the basis of insufficient reliability in relation to the seriousness of the effects of a few low scores.
- More generally, local educators, parents, and taxpayers are dismayed to find some schools labeled as failures that they are certain are good schools—and they have considerable evidence to support their opinions. This anomaly suggests a need for more careful and specific criteria for determining "adequate yearly progress" and "failing schools." On the other hand, it should be mentioned that the penalties for failing schools are applied gradually, over years of attempts at remediation. Only after five years of unsatisfactory results do the major penalties take effect, for example, turning over the administration of the school to the state or to an educational management company.
- The most serious issue in the relationship of NCLB to the states may be the least vigorously discussed: Each state sets its own learning standards and determines the assessment of them. The variations in standards and assessments result in large-scale discrepancies among the states in what constitutes a satisfactory or a failing school (Center on Educational Policy, 2006).

So, State A shows a failure rate in grade four mathematics of 40 percent, while only 10 percent of State B's schools are unsuccessful in that subject. Because the standards, tests, and norms vary from state to state, one cannot say that State B is doing a better job of teaching its students math than is State A. That the definition of an adequate grasp of mathematics should depend on the state in which a student lives is difficult to uphold, even by the most vociferous defenders of local control of learning standards, curriculum, and assessment.

The disparity among state achievement standards is dramatically shown by comparing scores on tests devised and scored by individual states with scores on the National Assessment of Educational Progress (NAEP) examinations in those same states. For example, in fourth grade reading in 2005, 39 percent of California's students were "proficient" on the state's examination, while NAEP results showed 21 percent were proficient. New York's state test classified 64 percent of its students as proficient, while NAEP termed 34 percent proficient. Mississippi stated that 87 percent of its fourth graders were reading at a proficient level; NAEP said that 18 percent were. Other startling contrasts are seen in Illinois, which considers 60 percent of its fourth graders to be proficient readers, while NAEP gives that rating to just 29 percent. Virginia claims a proficiency rate in fourth grader reading of 81 percent;

NAEP says 39 percent. A rare example of congruence was Missouri: both state and NAEP tests found 34 percent to be at a proficient level (Saulny, 2005).

These state-to-state disparities are highlighted in a statement from the U.S. Department of Education (Lewin, 2007). In that news story, Education Secretary Margaret Spellings is quoted as saying that "It's way too early to conclude we need to adopt national standards." Politically, it may always be too early for national standards, but for parents in states like California, New York, or Mississippi, who are being misled by results of their state exams, it is obviously much too late.

Professional educators have been passionately engaged in the debate over the merits of NCLB. Generally, those who defend a more traditional approach to schooling favor the assessment and accountability requirements of the law. Typically, these educators recognize and urge the remediation of the flaws in the Act, but perceive the demands for achieving reading and math proficiency in all students to be an obligation of justice, as well as a key to future learning and, finally, to national prosperity. However, the law doesn't lack for critics, especially among teachers' unions and school administrators; some professors in schools of education are among the most vocal opponents of NCLB, focusing especially on the validity of the mandated tests. Given the enormous disparity in state definitions of proficiency, the professors raise an important query: Are some of the reading and math tests really measuring proficiency in reading and math?

To a great extent, the secretary of the federal Department of Education is caught in a crossfire. "[Secretary] Spellings took a hard line, refusing to allow states to deviate from NCLB's directions." But, "Spellings has even been willing to reverse her own policies on NCLB . . ." (Davis, 2007). Predictably, each position drew fire from critics of the Act.

According to The Center on Education Policy (2006), the NCLB has had these effects in most states and schools districts:

1. Districts are doing a better job of aligning classroom teaching with state standards.
2. Principals and teachers are making better use of test results to improve teaching.
3. Scores on state tests are higher in the majority of states and districts.
4. Teachers report high stress levels and poor staff morale because of pressure to improve scores.
5. Most districts are cutting back on social studies, science, art, or other subjects to make more time for reading and mathematics.
6. The effects on achievement gaps between various groups are unclear.

Thus, the imposition of NCLB on states has resulted in some grinding gears and shooting sparks. It's beyond the scope of this book to draw up a set of solutions that would resolve all friction between federal and state regulations over student assessment and the uses of assessment results. We will, however, point out certain principles and a few conditions that teachers and administrators might bear in mind in any serious discussion about resolving the federal–state conflicts over their respective roles in student assessment.

Federal versus State Regulations

1. By default, the Constitution gives to the individual states the power to regulate public education. State legislatures, departments of education, and state and local school boards overcame their reluctance to concede any element of control when they accepted federal funds for earmarked purposes in schools (the Elementary and Secondary Education Act of 1965 is an example). Tax funds carry with them an element of accountability, and accountability implies control. However, for better or worse, the states have successfully fended off recommendations for a common curriculum and a comprehensive assessment process encompassing all states.

2. Consider the realities of politics and power. Like all political bodies, state legislatures and education departments, as well as local school boards, defend their turf. Their rallying cry of "local control" reverberates with Americans concerned about the overcentralization of power in Washington. Less persuasive is the argument that each state's students are best served by a set of learning standards and the assessment thereof that are designed by and for that state alone.

   Each state's standards look pretty much like those in other states. Often, these similarities derive from the general nature of the standards' requirements; these statements may reflect goals that everyone can accept without specifying the curricular content required to meet the goals. But shouldn't we expect states to have common standards *and* curricula? Do students in Oregon or Arkansas need to know more or less or different mathematics than those in Florida or Connecticut?

3. The greatest political stumbling block to more uniformity on what students need to know in K–12 education is not a uniform curriculum, but a *common assessment*. The reluctance to initiate such a standard is understandable. Results of tests that are common across all states would allow us to infer that 50 percent of the state school systems are below average! Understandably, legislatures and departments of education in that lower half believe that such a ranking could reflect badly on them. If student test results show which states are meeting high levels of achievement and which are lagging the field, the pride and pleasure taken by those in the "high achievement" category

will probably not equal the political pain suffered by legislators and educators in states that are labeled "low achievers." Basically, this fear is similar to the one raised by opponents of classroom testing: Some students will score higher than others and the others will feel bad.

The feelings of our state officials and school children who do poorly on tests are amply justified. Those feelings should prompt them to increase their efforts to boost achievement. They deserve support from educators and government at all levels; their shortcoming should not induce them or us to stick our heads in the sand and deny reality.

4. The National Assessment of Educational Progress (NAEP) is as close as the United States comes to a single, nationwide assessment of student learning. NAEP's schedule of examinations permits assessment in a given subject like reading or science to be administered only every few years, and only to a sample of students. Therefore, it cannot be used to judge the status or progress of individual students or small units of the student population.

The program does, however, allow certain comparisons of achievement between states and of changes in scores at various grade levels over several years. The standards on which NAEP bases its assessments and the assessments themselves are set by a board of educators; remarkably few complaints have been heard about the quality of NAEP examinations, or that they are seriously incompatible with states' standards.

5. However, the state-by-state *results* of the NAEP exams definitely do not resemble one another. That disparity in student achievement is not something that many legislatures and educators in the lower scoring states want publicized; it raises politically toxic questions about the quality of schools and the validity of state tests. Yet there are examples of state school systems, especially in southern states like South Carolina and Florida, that have faced the implications of low student test scores and made substantial and successful efforts to improve the quality of learning in their schools.

6. If states and school districts are to provide student assessments that meet appropriate standards of mental measurement, several conditions are essential: (a) What is tested must reflect what is taught in classrooms; what is taught in classrooms must reflect state standards. (b) A national definition of "proficient" performance in every course and grade level must be set by educators and measurement specialists, who would be obliged to justify any significant variations among states. (c) Accountability for results must be based on reliable measures of student gains, not specific score levels. (d) Test preparation must be curriculum-based, that is, not involving protracted drills on specific items, but focused on the content areas of the state standards.

(e) State assessments must be useful to schools and students; score results should be timely and contain information that helps administrators and teachers improve their curricula. (For elaboration, see P. E. Barton's *Unfinished Business*, 2004.)

THE BENEFITS AND DRAWBACKS OF MANDATED TESTING

How have state-mandated tests affected the 95,000 schools throughout the United States? Given that number, the only possible answer is, "in various ways." Because federal and state regulations have defined pass/fail scores for schools, those schools in which a substantial number of students are not meeting the prescribed level of achievement or are not making adequate progress toward that goal can be seriously affected. What are the benefits from state-mandated assessments? What are the unsatisfactory elements in state and federal regulations?

1. By setting standards for teaching and learning, states have reasserted their constitutional right to regulate public education. State-mandated standards say, in effect, that certain knowledge, skills, and attitudes are important for all public school students in the state to learn. Local school boards are left considerable freedom to decide how their curricula will satisfy those minimal state standards.

2. Given the status of standards as the "law of the state," officials in state departments of education needed to learn how well the standards were being implemented. So, statewide assessments became inevitable. Have these assertions of state control over schools been beneficial? We say, "In sum, yes."

3. There are good reasons for keeping governmental controls at the lowest practical level. However, for each of the 15,000 school boards in the United States to determine what is to be taught and how learning will be assessed would not only be inefficient, it would lead to inequities in learning standards even greater than now exist among the states. So the obligation for setting and measuring the achievement of standards falls to the next level of government, the states. Does the practice of allowing fifty states to set curriculum and assessment standards lead to educational inequities as well? Again, we say "Yes," but that's a more difficult issue to address, as public school governance is a legal prerogative of the states, not the federal government.

4. When state departments publish the results of their testing, the publication is usually accompanied by a ranking of schools in descending order of achievement. For some schools and districts, this practice is a great benefit. Communities with high achieving schools are desirable

places to raise children, so parents and real estate agents, along with school board members and school faculty, can rejoice in their success. But every school's enrollment cannot be like all students in the utopian district of Lake Woebegone: above average. Educators and most parents in low-scoring schools are usually well aware that their schools are deficient, but seeing that lowly status headlined in the local media rubs salt in the wounds.

The point of statewide assessment should not be to rank schools or label them as "good" or "bad" but to recognize (and analyze and describe) schools that are making progress while indicating what low-scoring schools need to do in order to improve. Certainly, such actions are potentially beneficial to schools and students.

Often, the response on the part of boards and school officials is "We need more money." More funding may indeed result in an increase in helpful resources and achievement gains, but the plea for greater funding can say, in effect, "We don't need to change our administration, or curriculum, or teaching; our students do not achieve well because we're an impoverished district."

5. The immediate effects of low test scores on local educators are complex, but discouragement is a normal reaction. Some disparage the test results as unimportant or as offering an incomplete view of student progress. Often with some justice, others point to conditions in their students' homes or communities that inhibit student achievement.

6. But there are teachers, boards, and states—Florida, Texas, Virginia, Massachusetts, North and South Carolina, for example—that accepted low test scores as a challenge, then implemented steps that have led to improvements. Note, however, that some states show wide gaps between state norms and those of NAEP, prompting questions about the "real" status of learning in those states.

The willingness of some states to hold their schools accountable for student learning has clearly benefited students in those states. Some of these states, Florida, for example, permitted students in "failing schools" to transfer out of them even before the NCLB Act mandated this transfer option. (A decision by Florida's Supreme Court threw out the provision that allowed students to transfer, at taxpayers' expense, to nonpublic schools.) Most parents, legislators, and at least some educators perceive such transfer options as beneficial. Boards, administrators, and teachers in the designated failing schools usually do not agree, arguing that the state and local authorities should concentrate on assisting schools with low-achieving student populations to succeed, rather than allowing students and the tax funds that accompany them to move to other schools.

NCLB STANDARDS AND PROVISIONS

The NCLB of 2001 is a huge, sprawling bill—some 680 pages incorporating more that fifty federal education programs; it attempted to bring about many fundamental changes in U.S. schools. We are concerned here with reviewing only the elements of the bill that relate to assessment. Thus the Act's provisions for "fully qualified teachers," tutoring, reading instruction, and so on, will not be discussed in this text. For information on the many provisions of the Act, see the presentation by Hess and Petrilli (2006). Bear in mind that the Act is due for renewal in Congress in 2008, and that renewal will surely include some changes, especially in provisions for assessment.

1. The NCLB's goal of all students in all states reaching proficiency in reading and math (and science) by 2014 is so unrealistic that it can cause otherwise well-disposed educators to question the viability of the entire Act. In recent NAEP exams, no state was even close to 100 percent proficiency. Given that state assessment standards are more lax than NAEP's, the fundamental goal of NCLB remains more as an ideal than as a practical objective.

2. The NCLB's definition of "failing schools" exemplifies both the benefits and the drawbacks of the bill. By requiring that state assessments show adequate yearly progress for subgroups that often lag in achievement, the Act does not allow schools and districts to hide behind averages in achievement. This insistence on the importance of all children learning is admirable and could contribute to narrowing the enormous achievement gap between white and Asian students on the one hand, and African Americans, Hispanics, and Native Americans on the other.

3. But the minimum number of students in each subgroup that can trigger a "failing" rating for a school is too low to justify such a high-stakes decision. Given the limitations of test reliability, the use of average test scores to determine success or failure can result in mislabeling schools that are close to the pass/fail boundary. One regrettable result of these limitations is a loss of confidence in the fairness of the Act itself, as educators and parents occasionally are bewildered to learn that their local school, which has shown overwhelming evidence of success on many criteria, is deemed a failure. Even an insufficient participation of a subgroup of students on the day of the test can lead to a misleading label of failing.

4. For years, states and local districts have adopted standards and, more recently, have instituted assessments of how well schools are meeting those standards. NCLB has added to those curriculum guidelines and

assessments a third element of evaluation, that is, decisions based on the data from assessments, as a few states have done for themselves.

The Act bluntly tells public schools that don't meet the criteria for adequately educating their students to improve or close their doors, a common requirement for charter schools. The decision to hold consistently failing schools accountable for their lack of success, to provide assistance to such schools for a limited period of probation, and to close schools whose students still do not meet minimal learning expectations powerfully focuses the attention of administrators and teachers in those schools. Surely, factors other than the quality of teaching can contribute to a school's poor performance. But whatever the causes of failure, NCLB insists that all children must learn. If, over time, students in a given school do not make progress, they will be transferred to a different school. That may be simplistic and sometimes can be unfair to teachers and administrators who labor in low-achieving schools, but making student progress the criterion for a school's success seems to make inherent good sense.

SUMMARY

- Various societal factors, especially affluence and poverty, correlate strongly with indicators of academic achievement like test scores and dropout rates. The correlation of wealth and academic achievement speaks to impediments that can influence achievement, but are not, of themselves, the principal causes of or obstacles to students' academic achievement.
- There is some positive correlation between a district's resources and its student test scores, but many inner-city schools with consistently poor records of student achievement are relatively well funded. Conversely, some modestly funded schools have demonstrated success with disadvantaged populations.
- Successful schools in educationally disadvantaged districts commonly adjust their curricula—what and how they teach—to the learning needs of their students. These schools also strongly encourage active parental support for school rules regarding students' behavior and study.
- Public schools are and should be political, that is, they should be governed by the standards and regulations of the state and forthcoming about the results of their teaching.
- The No Child Left Behind Act adds to state standards and assessments penalties for failing to meet those standards. These penalties, and the test results that trigger them, are major elements of controversy in the educational community.

2

The Basics of Assessment

Please read this chapter carefully! It's true that "statistics words" like *validity* and *reliability*—not to mention *correlation, coefficients,* and *standard error*— can bring a glaze to our eyes. But a grasp of some of these concepts is essential for understanding and using classroom and standardized assessment. Our intent in this chapter is to address the basic qualities of mental measurement that teachers need if they are to understand measures of student progress and make good use of the results of their assessments.

When teachers appraise their students' academic achievement, they are gathering data on their students' mastery of the knowledge, skills, and attitudes that are important in their courses. Why do they want this information? Primarily, so that after the teachers have evaluated the assessment data, they can help students take the next steps in learning. So, the overarching principle is: *Good assessment is appropriately valid, reliable, and efficient.*

THE THREE BASIC QUALITIES

The first building block in good assessment is *validity*. A test is valid to the extent that it measures what it is supposed to measure; in a chemistry test, one expects to find questions that deal with chemistry, and only with chemistry. The practical question regarding validity is "What inferences will I draw, what decisions can I make based on the results of my assessment?" So validity refers not only to what is measured, but to how the results are used.

"Good assessment is appropriately valid" sounds rather ambiguous. But there are more and less appropriate ways to use assessment results. A comprehensive, end-of-semester exam that weighs heavily on a student's final grade should provide convincing evidence of validity. In high-stakes testing, when students will be promoted or retained, or when a school will be judged as successful or failing, validity must be strong and clear. That is, the assessment must:

One, adequately sample the knowledge domain of the material,
Two, accomplish that task at an appropriate level of difficulty, and
Three, ensure that the resulting data is used in an appropriate and ethical manner.

If, for example, a mathematics test for fourth graders includes many lengthy word problems, the exam becomes, in part, a reading test. To that extent it is invalid for determining how much math students know, especially for students with limited English and/or reading proficiency. If the math exam includes problems in calculus, it is scarcely a valid measure for fourth graders—unless one is teaching a remarkably advanced group of fourth graders. If an exam concentrates only on a few elements of the course, it would be invalid to use the results for major decisions about student grades or placement. (See also our discussion on reliability, which follows.)

Finally, if the environment in which an examination is administered is disruptive, or if a student has a serious problem, for example, illness or emotional trauma, the results of the exam are probably invalid for the affected student.

Let's try to define this basic quality of appropriate validity with a few more examples.

Ms. Walters wants to assess her third graders' achievement in reading comprehension. Her test consists of twenty-five words or phrases for which students are to choose primary and secondary meanings. Is that an appropriately valid test? Valid for what? The response depends on the answer to questions like these: What inferences can Ms. Walters draw? What decisions will she make based on her twenty-five-item test results? Will students' scores on this test weigh heavily in determining their final grade in reading? Will she decide her next steps in reading instruction, or which students should join various reading groups, on the basis of the test outcomes? A twenty-five-item vocabulary test is inadequate to support such decisions, so it is an invalid test of reading comprehension in relation to such important issues and uses.

Is such a test useless? Not at all. It provides some information about an important element of reading comprehension. Teachers gain an understanding of their classes' and individual students' reading skills by accumulating many such observations. Individually, these assessments, like the test in question, homework assignments, listening to a student read, or posing questions to the class on the theme of a short story, may not be substantial enough to make valid inferences of reading achievement; but, *cumulatively*, they can provide as good or better a measure of students' progress than a single examination, however comprehensive and well designed.

Teachers can make valid inferences about complex skills like students' reading or math abilities by using multiple written assessments *in conjunction with* the teachers' own frequent and less formal observations of their students' achievement, even though any single one of those observations is only modestly valid.

Here's another example, to which some teachers may take exception. In Ms. Maxim's ninth grade science exam, she asks students to write a paragraph explaining covalent bonding, ionic bonding, and metallic bonding. She will deduct points from students' test grades for errors in spelling and grammar, or for lack of neatness.

So, what's the problem? Again, it's a validity issue. The test purports to assess students' understanding of an important element in chemistry; to be valid, the scores should reflect that intent. If Ms. Maxim were administering a language arts exam, she could validly probe students' abilities in grammar or spelling. But a score on a science test should reflect only what a student knows about science. Yes, like most teachers, we authors have despaired over students' errors in grammar and spelling and sloppy exam papers that make more difficult a task that, at best, requires considerable time and energy. These flaws in students' papers should always receive a comment and repeat offenders should be required to recopy their papers in readable form, or be otherwise penalized. Alternatively, teachers may choose to give a separate grade for spelling, grammar, and neatness. We present more about this topic in part IV: Grading and Reporting.

Another characteristic of good assessment is *reliability*. Reliability refers to the consistency of assessment results; as such, reliability may be a quality of students' performance or of the assessments themselves. Elana's scores on five weekly quizzes are 95, 91, 87, 93, and 62. The first four scores confirm her teacher's impressions of Elana's level of knowledge and skills. What might account for the last, discrepant score?

Let's begin with the obvious: perhaps Elana studied for the first four tests but not for the last one. Or she missed class the day the material on the final quiz was covered. Or she was just having a bad day.

But it's also possible that the test, not the student, is the problem. First, the number and variety of the questions may be inadequate for a student to show what she knows. There is also an issue of the quality of items asked in the exam. Every exam is a sample from a much larger domain of knowledge and skills; some elements are of greater importance than others in achieving the course objectives. In the first four quizzes, the questions dealt with issues that the teacher had defined as important, and the exam items largely corresponded to what Elana had studied.

In the fifth quiz, several of the questions did not match Elana's knowledge of the material. "Well, fine," her teacher says, "that's what tests are designed to do, to find out what students know or don't know." True, but some elements of a course are more important to know than others. If Elana's scores were usually low, if she normally demonstrated about a 60 percent grasp of the instructional material, her results on the final quiz would be no surprise, and one could confidently use that low score as part of her evaluation and assign an overall grade. But Elana consistently has shown a strong grasp of the important elements of the course, with a 92 percent average over the first four quizzes. In fact, the score of 62 may correctly reflect Elana's knowledge of the material covered in that test; if the items Elena missed were important ones, the results on her final quiz certainly could be used in calculating her average for the grading period.

But as an overall measure of her ability, Elana's low score is notably inconsistent with her usual work. Her teacher should at least review the quality of the test itself. If the items Elana, and perhaps other good students, missed measure trivial facts or abilities, if the questions are confusing or poorly worded, or if the material was not covered adequately in class, the test itself is invalid, unreliable, and thus unfair to students.

Still another teacher-based cause for unreliable scores is the failure to provide clear directions or to allow enough response time. These impediments to students accurately demonstrating the true level of their achievement also make the assessment invalid to a greater or lesser extent. An assessment that is unreliable is also invalid, that is, if a test does not reliably measure a student's ability, it is not doing what it purports to do.

It's important that, in drawing a sample of questions for a test, a teacher give his students many opportunities to display their knowledge. Of course, that's not always possible on a brief quiz, but over an entire grading period, teachers should give numerous assessments that incorporate various forms of academic measurement, such as short answers, essays, oral presentations, projects, and homework. In making an overall evaluation of students' achievement, teachers should allow for even the strongest students' occasional failure to perform well; teachers should ensure that both their high-achieving and their low-achieving students have many opportunities to demonstrate what they know and can do.

Why are validity and reliability so important in assessment? Because the quality of the assessment and the learning it tests depend on them, accountability, which is a responsibility of all educators, cannot be satisfied without assessment instruments and processes that are valid and reliable.

The third basis of good measurement is *efficiency*, a quality of educational assessment that is not always given sufficient consideration. An assessment is efficient to the extent that it yields useful results with the least demand on students' and teachers' time.

Mr. Lejane teaches a U.S. history course; he wants to assess his students' grasp of the recently studied Civil War. He could pose many questions about the causes, the events, the personalities, and the outcomes of that complex conflict. He might ask for several well-developed essays on some of these topics. To ensure that he covered every major topic in considerable depth, he would need many short-answer and recognition-type items. The resulting exam would be a thing of beauty, highly valid and reliable. Total testing time: four to five hours. Total time for him to grade the papers: We don't want to think about it.

Efficiency in an assessment simply means striking a balance between coverage of the important material and observing the constraints of students' and teachers' time and energy while still ensuring satisfactory validity and reliability. Teachers can then make adequate, if imperfect and partial, judgments of their students' achievement. Consider these examples of decisions about efficiency in assessments.

Our history teacher, Mr. Lejane, wants to determine whether students can place major events and personalities within fifty-year time periods. Should he use essays? Multiple-choice questions? Short answers? Our answer is: none of the above. For the factual information he is seeking, Mr. Lejane can ask more questions, gaining reliability in the process with less time required for preparing and scoring the items, by asking one or more matching questions, each with some ten items. (See part II for more on relating item types to the purposes of assessment.)

Ms. Christie is proud of basing an important part of assessment in her math class on "real life" problems like figuring interest on a multiyear loan or calculating measurements for remodeling a house. In the interest of efficiency should she drop these "context" problems and simply use the numbers and formulas? We say, "No." As long as the problems don't become time-consuming tests of reading skills, Ms. Christie should continue to make instruction and assessment in her math classes both interesting and practical.

OTHER MEASUREMENT TERMS

Besides the "basic basics" of validity, reliability, and efficiency, a few other statistical procedures can help us understand our students' test results.

Correlation is a measure of the relationship of one set of measures to another. A positive correlation means that the higher one stands on one measure, the higher he stands on another. Height and weight, for example, tend to be positively correlated, although not perfectly so. Scores on tests of vocabulary and writing skills tend to correlate positively, but again, the relationship will not be a perfect one, as there are variables other than vocabulary that affect a student's writing.

A negative correlation means that the higher one stands on one measure, the lower he stands on another. An example is the relationship between the number of errors on a math test and a teacher's grade on that test: the higher the number of errors, the lower the grade.

Standard error: Suppose that, for a vocabulary test, a teacher randomly selects 40 of the 1,500 words for which she wants her students to be able to supply, or at least to recognize, their definitions. The next day, she gives her class another test of 40 randomly selected items. Few, if any students in her class will earn exactly the same score on both tests. The variation that depends on the sample chosen is what standard error means.

It's a rare student who knows everything that a teacher can ask about a subject. The extent to which test items match a given students' knowledge leads to variations in the scores students receive. The standard error gives us a number on a score scale that tells us approximately how much variance from the given score we should anticipate. For example, if a student's grade on a 100-point scale is 85, a standard error of five means that the chances are two in three that his "true score" is somewhere between 80 and 90.

But to the variance by chance in the selection of items, we must add other sources of error in determining a student's true score: our own biases in choosing the questions for an exam, our mistakes in preparing and scoring the tests, and possible external conditions in the lives of our students—for example, illness, a quarrel with another student, and the like.

The reasons cited for interpreting cautiously the results of a single assessment indicate why it's so important that we employ *multiple measures* of assessment over a period of time before we make a global judgment about a student's achievement. The elements that contribute to error in test scores also encourage the use of *score bands*. Instead of assigning a specific numerical score, a score band extends one standard error above and one below the obtained score, as in our example. This procedure is a common and useful feature of many standardized test reports. The lesson of the standard error is that we should be wary of attributing too much precision to a single score, even one on a carefully designed test.

We'll mention just one additional measure that is frequently encountered when reviewing test scores, the *percentile rank*. This number is the percentage of student scores that fall below an individual student's score. For example, on a standardized mathematics test, Keisha's percentile rank is 85 percent. That percentage means that she scored better than 85 percent of the students in her norms group, that is, those with whom she's being compared. Note that a percentile rank simply compares a student with all the others in a group. It says nothing about how much of the subject a student has mastered.

For definitions of other statistical terms used by educational researchers, please see the glossary.

TWO BASIC QUESTIONS

Two basic questions teachers should ask as they prepare to assess their students are:

> One, why am I giving this assessment? That is, what's my purpose? What do I want to learn about my students' achievement? What will I do with the results?
>
> Two, specifically, how can I use the results to further student learning?

Let's assume agreement with the proposition that a teacher who does not in some way assess student learning, cannot teach successfully. Without information about how much of the skills and knowledge that have been taught have, in fact, been learned, a teacher cannot know what to teach next. Of course, one could forge ahead on the theory that "I give them the material; it's the students' obligation to learn." Such a teacher should either be retrained or encouraged to consider another profession.

Some may respond to the question of why they give an assessment by saying, "Because it's the end of the grading period," but that's not what the question is meant to elicit. Let's first consider some *bad* reasons for administering an exam.

"Many of you (students) are not paying attention in class, so tomorrow we'll have a quiz on the week's assignments." The groans that greet this announcement suggest that the potential test-takers don't want to be tested, a natural enough response; there is also a strong hint that the test is a punitive measure for less than satisfactory classroom behavior. It's true that a looming exam can focus at least some students' attention on what they should have learned. It's also true that in the best of school worlds, students will keep up with their coursework because they love learning. But that's not how many students in most classrooms behave.

There's nothing wrong with motivating students to study; regular assessments, planned and announced well in advance, can contribute to that stimulus. But teachers who use the threat of impromptu testing as a club for punishing student behavior generate ill will and, probably, more unsatisfactory behavior.

In considering *good* reasons for assessing students' academic progress, a teacher might answer one or several of the following questions:

1. What does my class as a whole and what do individual students understand about the important information and ideas that we covered this week, or in this grading period?
2. Can my students apply what they learned? Can they link it to prior learning? Can they evaluate issues or problems, using what they have learned?

3. What do the results of assessment tell me about the effectiveness of my instruction? Should I re-teach some concepts? Should I be moving faster with all or some of the class?
4. Should some students be considered for placement in a class that is more or less advanced? Do some students need tutoring assistance?
5. Can I be reasonably sure that the grades I assign to students fairly represent their achievement in my class?
6. Is it time to stop and review what my class has studied in the last week or month? If teachers schedule periodic assessments and prepare for them by reviewing important points in class, students are likely to study more, with a sharper focus and better results.

Our second basic question is: how can assessment help students learn? Again, let's first consider a few ways that assessment does *not* help students learn.

First, measures that are invalid or unreliable for their purposes can only yield flawed results, leading to faulty inferences about students' achievement by their teachers and, perhaps, by the students themselves.

Second, a few teachers say to students or parents that tests, especially standardized tests, are not important. However intended, such comments tell students that that they need not bother to do their best on the assessments in question. This comment misleads both students and parents. Most classroom tests are important; some tests are critically important in determining whether a child is retained in a grade, or whether a school is labeled as failing by a state department of education.

Third, the opposite fault is to overemphasize the importance of a test. Some students and parents apparently believe that an upcoming examination can decide their children's fate forever, or at least for the next four years. The high level of anxiety this attitude generates detracts from students' performance on the test. If the importance of a test score is exaggerated, all parties are misled about the significance of a single measure of academic achievement. The classic example of this last problem is the anxiety that precedes the administration of college admission tests and the interpretations students, parents, and, sometimes, school officials place on their results.

Companies that sell the tests, and organizations and individuals that coach students for the tests, have an obvious interest in emphasizing their importance. College admissions officials usually insist that scores on the SAT or ACT are "only one factor" in the acceptance of students to selective colleges. Judging from the enormous amount of time and money spent on coaching students for their college entrance exams, that assurance doesn't seem to alleviate parental and student anxiety or to slow the rush to enroll in test preparation classes.

But enough of negatives; let's look at how assessment *can* enhance student learning. All of the items below apply to teachers' own classroom tests; some can also be used with standardized tests.

First, what can teachers do *before or during* an important assessment, for example, a final exam?

1. Several days before the exam, explain the type of questions that will appear on the exam, how students are to respond, and how much time will be given for the entire test. During the administration, give one or two reminders of how much time remains and about how many questions students should have completed.

2. Review the important learning that will be sampled in the test. Point out key material in the text, class notes, homework, projects, and other assignments. Tell your Spanish class, for example, "You will be asked to translate three short paragraphs from the past semester's reading and to answer several questions about the texts, for example. . . . You will not be required to translate passages from English to Spanish, but there will be a section of English words and phrases for you to translate into Spanish."

3. Before major tests, give students examples of each type of item that will appear on the exam. "Walk through" the examples, showing students how to attack the questions most efficiently. This rehearsal is especially important for elementary school students. When an exam includes one or more essay questions, give an example of an essay question with appropriate directions, then ensure that students understand what constitutes a good response. (See part II, chapters 4, 5, and 6 for various types of exam questions.) Ask students how they would approach each of the item types; the teacher can then approve, expand on, or correct student responses.

4. "Give away" one or a few items on the exam by saying, for example, "One of the following three topics will be an essay question," or, even more explicitly, "I will ask you to explain in a paragraph why Great Britain became a dominant world power during the nineteenth century." (This applies to classroom tests only.)

   That last suggestion may sound counterintuitive, but test-takers, especially those most seriously challenged, are encouraged by seeing a question they know they can answer. And in thinking about and writing the answer, students can better learn an important element of the course.

5. Explain efficient ways of studying for and taking the exam. Differences in students' grades derive not just from general intelligence or even knowledge of the subject, but can reflect the study skills students have mastered. These competencies are learnable and should be explained

and practiced in class. Good teachers want their students to demonstrate that they have mastered the most important information and skills taught in the course. When a student fails to do so because of factors unrelated to the content of the test, the results of the exam are of doubtful validity for that student. Basic test-taking skills are easily taught: careful reading of directions, keeping track of time, checking answers, among others, can assist students in giving valid responses, that is, responding to the test to the best of their ability.

6. Let the students prepare the test. Objection: "They'll know the answers and all will receive high scores." Stop! Go back to "Why am I giving this assessment?" Is it to discriminate, or to engender winners and losers among my students? To create a bell curve of scores? In standardized tests, that is commonly the intent, and distinguishing the students at the extremes of achievement, as well as the great majority in the middle, can serve a legitimate educational purpose.

But assessment is a means to another end; the primary purpose of classroom assessment should be to enhance student learning. Let students identify and argue over the major elements of the course that should be represented on an exam. Let them formulate questions for that test. Ask those who create the questions to prepare model answers. Then administer the assessment pretty much as students have fashioned it. No, that exam should not be the only assessment in a grading period. But involving students in designing the assessment can contribute substantially to student learning, the ultimate purpose of the class.

7. Perhaps a teacher's most important contribution to successful student assessment is communicating an expectation and a *desire* that every student do well on a test, or over a grading period. Tests are not part of the curriculum to enable teachers to demonstrate their authority or control. They are an important element of students' learning experiences, and teachers want their students to learn. That's why teachers should do all they can to help students do their best on all measures of learning.

What can teachers do *after* an exam to enhance student learning? (Numbers 2 through 4 are applicable to standardized test results if teachers receive an item analysis.)

1. Grade tests, homework, and projects and review them in class as soon as possible. Teachers are obliged to tell students as soon as possible the results of their tests, projects, homework, and other assessments and give them an opportunity to learn from them. When many days or even weeks go by without feedback, students become progressively

less interested in the content of the assessments, or in how well they did. They are also likely to repeat and reinforce errors from the exam in other assignments unless their mistakes are corrected promptly.

2. During the posttest review in class, place the questions and responses in the context of the course. Why is this question important? How does each question relate to prior learning, or to what lies ahead in the course?

3. If students show deficiencies in important material, use the test questions as a homework assignment; ask students to hand in papers with every response correct.

4. Note carefully any question that many of the ablest students got wrong. Ask yourself, "Was the question ambiguous or otherwise unclear?" "Did I cover this material adequately in class?" "Should I reteach some of this material?"

ROLES IN ASSESSMENT

Another basic issue in assessment is clarifying who is responsible for what. Obviously, students and teachers are critically involved in classroom and standardized assessment. Additionally, parents, administrators, and school board members have roles to play in selecting or preparing assessment instruments, in their administration, or especially, in reporting and using assessment results.

Note that these groups must frequently interact with one another: administrators discuss assessment strategies and the results of testing with their teachers; teachers explain the results of assessment to parents; the school board depends on its administrators for analyses of school or district assessment outcomes; and of course, students are at the center of all this activity. We suggest the following roles for those who participate in measuring student achievement and offer some thoughts on how those roles can be played productively.

1. Students: Their role is pretty straightforward, they take the tests. But as teachers know well, and other parties should remind themselves, almost no one, young or old, enjoys being assessed and evaluated. Let's consider some ways that the students' role in assessment can be made less painful and more productive for those most directly involved.

   Forgive this statement of the obvious, but the best way for students to moderate the pain and maximize the gain from tests is—study! The feeling that one is well prepared for an assessment can reduce pretest jitters, improve performance on the test, and induce a feeling of satisfaction in having given an exam their best shot. The more students know about an upcoming exam, the better they can prepare for it, so reducing students' anxieties and improving their performance depends heavily on teachers doing their part by preparing valid tests and clear directions for them.

Researchers support teachers' experience and commonsense about the importance of students' perseverance in studying (Duckworth and Seligman, 2005). The researchers reported higher test scores and grades for those students defined as "self-disciplined." They define that term as "doing what you have to do when you don't want to do it." The study also notes that the higher achieving students watch less television and spend more time on homework than their more impulsive peers.

A few other obvious recommendations: an examination that carries major consequences for grade point averages should be preceded by a good night's rest and a good breakfast or lunch. Teachers should, to the extent possible, avoid scheduling major tests for the day before or after the Big Game or the Spring Fling. But such planning errors sometimes occur. One can at least say that they give students a chance to make a choice; most will choose fun over study, but in the process, they may learn something about the good and bad consequences of choices and decisions.

2. Parents play an important role in students' academic success and, specifically, in how well their children perform on significant tests. Parents should try to steer a course between overemphasizing the importance of examinations and suggesting that school assessment and evaluation are trivial or inaccurate. Parents who say, in effect or literally, that their children's whole future rides on the results of an exam (consider college admissions test anxiety) are communicating several bad messages: "If you don't do (extremely) well, you will have failed (us)." If you don't score very well, you will not be able to. . . ." That parents may deliver such messages out of concern for their children's future does not lessen the harmful impact. Conversely, parents who are indifferent to their children's school assessments convey the message that such measures are unimportant.

What should parents do to help their children succeed on school examinations? First, be aware of important upcoming examinations; speak of them as opportunities to display students' achievement; demonstrate interest by insisting on appropriate preparation through study, without communicating anxiety about the results. Yes, that's a thin line to walk.

Second, ensure that children are rested and properly fed before heading off to the big exam. Pulling an all-nighter before an exam is a college tradition that parents sometimes unwisely boast of. For younger children especially, inadequate rest contributes mightily to anxiety and memory lapses. Third, parents provide a powerful lesson when they insist on reviewing important test results and grades on major projects and ascertaining that their children know the correct responses to all questions.

3. Teachers are in the driver's seat for most examinations, especially for those they prepare for their own students. Even for standardized tests, teachers often administer the exams and review the results for students and parents. Teachers should be the principal evaluators of their students' progress, not only because they give exams, but because they have day-to-day contact with students, observing and assessing them in a variety of ways. This long-term process of multiple observations allows teachers to make overall judgments of their students' academic achievement, as well as of other qualities and behaviors.

Teachers are fallible human beings; they will not invariably draw accurate, insightful inferences even from many samples of their students' assessments. But trained, experienced professional educators are the most reliable source for understanding students' academic achievement.

As teachers prepare for a major classroom assessment, they review the most important elements the exam will cover, explain their expectations for students responses, and indicate how much each item on the exam will "count." At the beginning of the exam period, teachers ensure that students understand the directions: how to respond to each type of question, how much time is allotted for the entire exam, and so on. They then move around the room, monitoring the process. Teachers who sit at their desks grading papers or leave the room during a test are inviting cheating by a few students: a bad lesson for all test-takers.

After promptly grading and returning the exam papers, teachers should review the items on the exam and provide, or have the class provide, the best responses to each question. This practice can correct erroneous information and reinforce the important learning appraised in the examination.

Note that under the "parent role" description, we urge parents to review the results of major exams with their children. As teachers ourselves, we authors admit to mixed feelings about this recommendation. Some parents, especially those in privileged suburban schools, will take issue with some exam questions and the scores assigned to their children's responses. The bottom line: Accept that overanxious parents will take some of your time, get a good grip on your patience and sense of humor, and then send home the papers. Maybe your phone or e-mail won't be contacted. Maybe.

As teachers prepare important examinations, they should remind themselves that they want all students to do their best. If a teacher prepares a good test of the important elements of the course, and every one of her students receives an A or B, so much the better. "But the administration insists that our grades differentiate among the higher and lower achieving students." If teachers use various means of assessment, including homework, class quizzes, student presentations, and portfolios, as well as several significant exams, grades in a typical classroom will begin to distribute themselves along a rough curve. Note that high school principals who complain about "too many high grades" are delighted if most of their Advanced Placement students receive high grades of 4 or 5 on the annual examinations.

Teachers are professionals; as such, they have certain basic obligations. One is to act always for the good of their students; another is to hold themselves accountable to the community, and especially to students and parents. To place the welfare of students first in assessment means using classroom assessment and, as possible, standardized tests to help all students learn. Accountability is the recognition that teaching is a serving profession; the community and parents entrust their children to their teachers. So, teachers owe to their students, parents, and the public clear explanations of how well they have succeeded in helping students learn.

4. Administrators contribute to the student assessment process in several ways, but their most important contribution is made well in advance of classroom testing. Prospective teachers sometimes receive very little instruction in their college courses about how to assess student achievement. Administrators should provide in-service training for their faculties in techniques of observation and questioning, and in how to design, administer, and use the results of classroom assessment. (See appendix B for an outline of such an in-service workshop.)

Administrators also should help teachers gain more information than most of them now have on preparing for, interpreting, and using the results of standardized examinations. Ideally, training sessions on classroom assessment should take place at or before the start of a school year; one or two follow-up sessions should also be scheduled, preferably just before major examinations. Teachers' preparation for administering and using results of standardized tests is most helpful immediately before the exams; training in using the exam results effectively is most helpful upon receipt of the results.

Standardized test scores are increasingly used to measure the academic success of teachers and schools, as well as classes, subgroups, and individual students. Whatever one thinks of the dependence on a single measure to make important judgments, it is a reality that demands the attention of administrators. Most superintendents, principals, and supervisors have some graduate training in mental measurement; they may need to brush up on standard deviations, confidence intervals, correlations, and such. (See the glossary for these and other assessment terms.) Administrators may need these and similar concepts in order to interpret the significance of standardized test scores to their communities, to their staffs, and to their boards and parents.

Administrators of individual schools should also be familiar with good practices in classroom assessment, and should routinely request copies of teacher-made assessments, preferably tests and assignments with teachers' comments and grades on them. This familiarity with teachers' assessment procedures is an important part of a local administrator's role in supervising instructional quality in schools. Classroom assessments show what teachers perceive to be the most important elements in their courses. The quality of the test items, the directions to students, and the grades and comments provide considerable information on teachers' skills in instruction and in classroom assessment.

5. School trustees do not assess students; nor should they be privy to individual students' scores. But, together with the chief administrator, board members should review carefully the results of student assessment at the grade, school, and district levels. Whatever the limitations of standardized testing, it offers boards and a community an all-too-rare opportunity to receive an objective, external evaluation of their students' achievement.

SUMMARY

- The basic principle: Good assessment is appropriately valid, reliable, and efficient.

The three basic qualities of good student assessment:

Validity: Does an assessment measure what it claims to measure? How will the results be used?

Reliability: Are students' results on a given examination consistent with other assessments of the same students? Is the test itself constructed properly?

Efficiency: Does an assessment yield adequate results with a minimum demand on teachers' and students' time?

The two basic questions:

Why am I giving this assessment? That is, how will my students and I benefit from it?

How can my assessments help students learn? That is, what can I do before, during, and after an assessment to enhance student learning?

- Roles in assessment: Students, teachers, parents, administrators, and trustees are all important players in selecting, administering, reporting, and evaluating the results of student assessment. Teachers bear the greatest professional responsibility for preparing, reporting, and using the results of assessment.

II

CLASSROOM ASSESSMENT

In part II, chapters 3 through 6, we continue with our aim of making the material as convenient and useful as possible for teachers. We first address the three purposes teachers have in mind when they assess their students: formative, summative, and diagnostic assessment. We then open the toolbox for assessment, indicating the various means teachers use to determine what their students have learned. We show how to prepare the questions, when each type of item can be used most effectively and efficiently, and what the limitations are for each item type.

Chapter 4 deals with *recognition* items: questions and problems for which the answer is made available to test-takers; their challenge is to recognize it. Recognition items include multiple-choice and matching items.

Chapter 5 covers *supply* items, from short-answer questions to restricted and extended essays. Again, we clarify when these item types should and should not be used, and how to prepare and score them.

In chapter 6, we describe *performance* assessment items. These are work samples that directly measure the skills being tested, for example, a behind-the-wheel driver's test, fashioning a sculpture in an art class, or conducting a chemistry experiment. We include in this chapter a section on portfolio assessment, which can be a collection of work in any subject. We conclude the chapter with comments on classroom observation as an assessment tool.

3

Formative, Summative, and Diagnostic Assessment

A REMINDER

Before getting into the nuts and bolts of classroom assessment, it may be useful to review quickly the principal points in chapter 2, The Basics of Assessment:

- All assessment should possess the basic qualities of validity, reliability, and efficiency, but in varying degrees, depending on how the results of the assessment will be used.
- The two basic questions teachers should ask as they plan any assessment are: "Why am I giving this assessment?" That is, what do I expect to learn about my students' knowledge and skills? The principal reasons or purposes are the subject of this chapter on formative, summative, and diagnostic assessments. The second question is, "How will I use the results of my assessment to improve student learning?"

These qualities and questions are the requisites of good assessment, which complements and supports good teaching.

FORMATIVE ASSESSMENT: PURPOSE AND PRACTICE

Formative assessment could be termed "informative assessment," as its purpose is to help students and teachers understand what students have learned and what they need to study next. Formative assessment does not usually yield grade reports or create other recorded evaluations of students. That's the role of summative assessment, which we will consider next. So, formative assessment can be quite informal, it may come from various brief measures, as long as it provides helpful information to teachers and students.

The core purpose of formative evaluation is to answer two fundamental questions teachers should pose. First, "Are my students learning what they should be learning?" This question implies that teachers have measurable learning objectives for the major elements of their curricula, that is, they know what their students should be learning. This principle is easy when teachers consider only facts, rules, definitions, and so forth. That level of learning is a necessary but partial intended result of virtually every course. So, "are my students learning?" asks not just what information they have accumulated, but also, "What can they *do* with their learning?" The second fundamental question for teachers is, "What can *I* do with this information?"

Formative assessment speaks to students' relationship to learning. The information allows teachers to focus both on the students' learning characteristics and on the learning itself. In teaching, there is a danger of assuming that once the content and methodologies are set for a course, the only variable teachers need to work with is the students. The curriculum and both content and teaching strategies are indeed set at the start of a course, but they are not set in concrete. Constant formative assessment allows teachers to consider not just what student have learned and still need to learn, but how teaching can be adjusted to facilitate that learning.

Let's look at a scenario where formative assessment can play an important role. Janet Smith is a sixth grade social studies teacher. Early in the school year, she is completing a unit on the Neolithic period. Her class first read about and discussed the role of archeology in revealing the distant past. The unit then dealt with such topics as hunter-gatherer peoples and pastoral cultures, among others. In one class period, students gave presentations in which they played the roles of various members of an early agriculture-based civilization. It's now time to move on with the study of other early civilizations.

The question for Ms. Smith is: are the students ready to move ahead, that is, have they mastered the principal elements of the unit on the Neolithic period, especially understandings they need in order to comprehend significant material in the next units? What does Ms. Smith have, and what does she still need, by way of assessment and evaluation to answer the question of whether to move on?

A common response to Ms. Smith's concern is to give a formal, written unit test. That gives her the information she desires, and the results can probably be used for summative purposes to contribute to students' grades in the course.

But by the time the test is prepared, administered, scored, and returned to students, Ms. Smith will be well into the next unit. Whether students are prepared to move on is a moot point; they have moved on, ready or not.

The students' role play gave Ms. Smith some formative assessment information. If, additionally, she had simply posed a few questions on important elements of the unit *every class day*, ensuring that she called on students with a range of abilities, Ms. Smith could be reasonably assured that her class was, or was not, ready to move on.

Basic Qualities

What then are the elements of formative assessment?

- It occurs at many points, even every day, within a class. In the example above, Ms. Smith is counting on her formal unit exam to answer her questions about how well the students have learned about the Neolithic period. But we, in our omniscience, immediately see her problem: By the time she knows what her students have and haven't learned, it's too late to do anything about it without breaking off the newly begun unit. Ms. Smith needs to begin asking "Are my students learning?" by the end of the first class. The results can be quickly evaluated.
- Unlike a full-scale unit test, formative assessment should yield rapid, almost immediate results. An obvious way to achieve that efficiency is to pose a few questions in class to a range of students. Perhaps once a week, a teacher can give a brief written quiz, using selection or short-answer items described in chapters 4 and 5. After the teacher collects the papers, a show of hands on responses the students chose allows for an immediate perception of where the class stands, and a prompt correction of errors. The teacher may then want to glance at the papers to confirm the responses student have selected, especially for those students who typically are most challenged in the class.
- It emphasizes the teacher's understanding of student learning, not specific grades or rank.
- The intent of formative assessment and evaluation is to inform teachers and students about what the latter have learned—period. It is a tool used primarily to adjust the curriculum to the needs of students. Formative assessment carries with it no penalties; it does not determine grades, promotion, or reports to school, state, or federal authorities.
- It can be used to adjust an individual lesson, even the content and teaching methods of an entire curriculum.
- Note that the adjustments mentioned in the previous sentence are all on the part of the teacher. Basically, the purpose of formative assessment is to "adjust" the students, that is, to improve their learning. But,

as teachers, we should approach our classes with a certain degree of humility about the effectiveness of our teaching. When students aren't learning despite our superb material and creative style of teaching, maybe, just maybe, the fault is not entirely theirs. The ability and willingness to search through our repertoire of knowledge and skills and come up with fresh approaches is the mark of a professional teacher.

- It emphasizes assessment *for* learning, not *of* learning.
- A recent text (Stiggins, 2004) eloquently argues that formative assessment is an integral element in the cycle of improving teaching and learning. The enhancement of lessons plans, even an entire course curriculum, can follow on a teacher's monitoring of and reflection on student learning. (See also part V on Program Evaluation.)

SUMMATIVE ASSESSMENT AND EVALUATION

As the term suggests, summative assessment sums up a number of factors and comes up with an evaluation: a finding, a judgment, a decision. When people speak of "tests," especially if the term is preceded by a derogatory adjective, they usually are referring to summative assessments: semester or end of course exams devised by classroom teachers, or standardized tests laid on by the district or state. What are the characteristics of summative assessments, and how do they differ from the formative assessments that teacher use?

Primarily, we define summative assessment through its intended purpose or by how the results will be used. For teachers' own summative testing, there are the periodic exams, whose scores will contribute significantly toward students' final grades and, perhaps, their promotion. Teacher-assigned papers and projects can also contribute to summative judgments of students' performance. Then there are the state-mandated examinations that can result in good news for a class, school, or district, or can lead to increased oversight and penalties for a school.

Summative exams that contribute to important decisions should be more complex and on a larger scale than teachers' formative assessments. They are longer—that is, they have more questions and a greater variety of test items—and they should demonstrate high levels of validity and reliability. Those requirements are especially critical when a decision is to be made on the basis of a single assessment's results—rarely a good practice.

Why do summative examinations require more testing time and employ a wider variety of test items than formative evaluation? Typically, summative exams measure a large swath of the curriculum, sometimes an entire course. For purposes of both validity and reliability, test questions should touch on most of the important learning that's being tested.

Let's consider Henry Wiggins as he plans his final exam in U.S. history. Mr. Wiggins began the year with chapters on our Native Americans and the earliest European discoveries in the new world and made it through the first Bush administration, so he has loads of material to choose from; admittedly, some of it was covered rather hurriedly. But at several points in the year, our teacher paused to review the salient elements in what went before; toward the end of the year, he distributed a four-page outline of people, events, and ideas that were most important in U.S. history. Two weeks before the classroom final exam, Mr. Wiggins assigned a topic for a take-home essay, due a few days before the in-class examination; the essay would count for one-third of the final exam grade. A week before the final, Mr. Wiggins told his class the kind of questions they would encounter on the rest of the final, and how best to respond to them. Then he prepared a test that included a substantial number of multiple-choice and matching items, as well as short-answer questions. He chose these item types to ensure that the test had a large number of items, making certain that it sampled as many important elements of the course as possible.

If Mr. Wiggins had heavily focused his exam on the colonial period, or if his questions were based disproportionately on the Civil War or on all wars the United States fought, the test's validity and reliability would be compromised; it would not fairly represent what was taught in the course. Note that Mr. Wiggins included an extended essay in his final exam. This type of question is especially desirable for allowing students to demonstrate the analytical and evaluative skills that are more difficult to probe with selection or short-answer items.

It's good to remind ourselves that, in summative assessment as in its more informal cousin, formative assessment, the teachers' goal is to help students learn. That objective can be lost when it's time to create an exam that contributes heavily to students' grades. Teachers may feel, and be told, that they should make major exams very rigorous, resulting in a wide distribution of scores throughout the class. But if a teacher has designed an exam based on the learning objectives of her course and most students score very well, isn't that what she, not to mention her students and their parents, want to see? In preparing for summative exams by reviews and discussing good responses to sample questions, and in following a major test with a class review of the questions and best responses, summative evaluation contributes to student learning. These remarks are not meant as an argument for diluting the content of examinations, but for ensuring that, one, students understand the principal knowledge and skills they are expected to learn and, two, that only important knowledge and skills are tested on a comprehensive exam.

DIAGNOSTIC ASSESSMENT: QUALITIES AND USES

We said that assessment is largely defined by the uses to which teachers put the results. Diagnostic assessment is usually formative in its form; its purpose is a narrow one, to focus on students with severe learning problems. These students, usually the lowest achieving in a class, require intervention, with careful assessment and planning for instruction if they are to be appropriately taught without consuming a disproportionate amount of classroom teachers' time.

Note that we are not speaking here of special education classes for students whose learning problems are so complex that they require specialized teachers in their own classrooms. These teachers are trained in the diagnostic procedures their students require. Almost every classroom teacher has a few students who don't seem to "get it" from the content and methods of the given curriculum. Many teachers have students who are "mainstreamed." These students often bring with them Individual Educational Plans (IEPs) that detail the objectives and expectations for the students. As we speak here of diagnostic assessment, we are referring to these teachers and students.

Diagnostic assessment focuses narrowly on specific learning difficulties of an individual or small group of students in a classroom. Early in the school year, Michael has already failed several math quizzes. He's told his teacher that "I'm no good in math," a statement that seems painfully accurate. He appears unable to work successfully with almost any element of the math curriculum. Why? At what point in a math problem does Michael err or, more often, give up? Sometimes, the answer is that a student has not grasped procedures or principles that are basic to further learning. For example, Michael never mastered some fundamentals of arithmetic, such as how to solve division problems, or how to work with fractions and decimals.

Some students can't follow instructions in class because they don't comprehend the vocabulary of mathematics, or they can't work through a problem at the same pace as others in a class because they have not memorized such basic elements as the multiplication tables. Diagnostic assessment and subsequent instruction can, to a limited extent, take place in the classroom, but they are most effective in one-on-one sessions. Tutoring sessions should begin as soon as a student's need is perceived, with assessments of the specific points at which a student begins to founder. If a tutor does not first assess the specific nature of a student's problem, instruction is likely to fail, thus giving a student further evidence that he's "no good at math."

A tutor begins by asking, "At what point does this student begin to lose the thread of instruction?" That is the point at which intensive instruction begins. One-on-one tutoring is an expensive use of teacher time. But it is less costly than allowing a student to move through school without having learned how to learn math. Because it is a highly cumulative subject, success in most mathematics courses depends on being able to use the knowledge and skills learned in earlier classes. Students who have not mastered basic math skills will fall further and further behind until, discouraged and humiliated, they drop out of mathematics classes as soon as they can. This failure to develop basic math literacy leads to high school dropouts and virtually guarantees that such students will not attend college.

Our references to tutoring convey our strong conviction that every school should have in place a system for and a team of tutors. Classroom teachers are often the best tutors, so a period should be built into every teacher's schedule for tutoring duties. If state laws permit retired teachers or other qualified persons to give an hour a day, they should be asked to serve. But finally, boards of education *must* budget for tutorial services.

A teacher with twenty-odd students in her class cannot devote intensive remedial instruction to one or a few of them. Certainly, good teachers make adjustments in their teaching for the varying abilities of their students. But if administrators and trustees intend to give appropriate instruction to their students who are most in need of prompt help, they must carve out time and allocate funds for systematic diagnostic assessment and remedial instruction. Districts that do not do so are failing their most vulnerable students and almost guaranteeing that those students will continue to fail throughout their schooling.

SUMMARY

- Formative assessment is "informative assessment," as it answers two important questions teachers ask: "Are my students learning what they should be learning?" and "How can I use the results of assessment to help students learn?"
- Formative assessment is frequent, and the results can be quickly evaluated and put to use. It emphasizes understanding and improving student achievement, not just giving grades, and it can help teachers adjust their teaching to their students' needs.
- Summative assessment is intended to "sum up" student progress: It can be a basis for grades and promotion. Thus summative assessments are typically lengthy and complex measures with a variety of item types; they must show strong evidence of validity and reliability.
- Diagnostic assessment focuses on the learning problems of one or a few students. This chapter does not address the diagnostic processes

used by special education teachers, who are trained in assessment techniques appropriate to the severe learning problems of their students; here we speak to diagnoses by teachers in standard classrooms. We plead the importance of systematic provisions in schools for diagnosing and tutoring students who are not making progress in their classes.

4

Selection Responses

Two topics precede our descriptions of various types of assessment items: one refers to the merits of diverse types of test questions; the other related topic is how to match test items with the knowledge and skills we want students to display. Both topics have particular relevance to this chapter on selection responses.

Selection items, primarily multiple-choice (MC) and matching questions, have a bad reputation among some educators; these items tend to be identified with standardized tests, which does not endear them to most teachers. "Students are just regurgitating facts, not thinking critically." "The answers are right in front of them, they don't have to know anything, they can guess the correct response." Neither of these objections is entirely true, nor entirely false.

Selection items are efficient ways to probe a student's store of information: facts, rules, names, dates and historical periods, events, locations, and so on. Students' ability to recall them does indeed call principally on their memories, although some understanding is usually required for the memory to function efficiently. That is, students are more likely to remember actions that Franklin Roosevelt took to alleviate the effects of the Great Depression if they understand the nature of that period and why Roosevelt was elected president in 1932. Of course, that understanding too could be termed "just information." "But," the objection goes, "asking students to recall information about Roosevelt and the Depression is not the same as asking them to think critically about Roosevelt's presidency or the economic slump of the 1930s."

That's true, and we authors declare ourselves firmly in favor of encouraging students to think critically. As former history teachers, we would enjoy hearing a class analyze the causes of the Depression, explain why some elements of Roosevelt's program succeeded and other didn't, and hypothesize the outcomes if a different program had been undertaken. A teacher who stimulates such a discussion can feel that special joy that is much of the reward of teaching: the pleasure of seeing students grow intellectually.

However, how can we think critically about a person, an event, or an idea without possessing considerable information about them? Yes, if Isabel knows only that Franklin Roosevelt was president during the Great Depression, and she has some general idea of what a depression is, she can offer her opinions or feelings about presidents or poverty. That's not critical thinking.

If acceptable contributions to classroom discussion or responses to examination questions consist of opinions unsupported by reality, that is, information relevant to the topic, students are being allowed to substitute uninformed assertions for critical thinking. As those deprived student progress in school, they will discover that unsubstantiated opinions and feelings are not acceptable responses in science, or critical reading, or art history, or any other discipline.

To connect the issue of thinking to this chapter on selection responses: Multiple-choice and matching items are primarily, though not exclusively, useful for testing students' store of information. It's true that such items can focus on trivia, rather than on significant facts, rules, and the like that students need to know. And it's a good guess that a teacher who tests for trivia teaches trivia. Student instruction and assessment should focus on significant knowledge, information that students need in order to learn more—and to think critically.

So, this long-winded defense of selection test items intends to make the point that these items have an important place in a teacher's assessment arsenal.

We should note that MC and matching items are not the only species of selection items. Rank-ordering a list of data according to temporal priority, importance, and so forth is another example. Gronlund (2006, pp. 103–8) describes the Interpretative Exercise, in which students read a paragraph of text, a complex math problem, a map, or other information, and then respond to a series of questions about the material they have read. This item type is increasingly familiar as more and more standardized tests emphasize critical reading: a text followed by several multiple-choice questions about the material. In this book we restrict our explanations to the most common selection items and, in later chapters, to the supply-type items most often used in classroom assessment.

Our second preliminary topic offers some recommendations we have found useful as we try not to rely only on recall of knowledge, but to vary the cognitive level of our test questions. Really, we do want to encourage critical thinking!

A key part of speech in every test item is the verb, what students are asked to *do* with the question. We have taken some liberties with B. S. Bloom's *Taxonomy*, both the original version (Bloom, 1956) and the revised edition (Anderson and Krathwohl, 2001), to recommend ways of improving the level of knowledge and skill that an item assesses by suggesting verbs that ask for specific levels of cognitive skills. Therefore, if you want to assess:

Knowledge, ask your students to describe, identify, list, match, name, recognize, select, define, recall.

Comprehension, ask them to classify, explain, distinguish, interpret, predict, summarize, understand, reword, translate, illustrate, demonstrate, conclude.

Application, ask students to compute, demonstrate, arrange, adapt, practice, modify, operate, solve, use.

Analysis, ask that they examine, diagnose, differentiate, diagram, estimate, infer, separate, order, distinguish, classify, categorize, deduce.

Evaluation, ask students to criticize, compare, contrast, rate, judge, justify, conclude, support, discriminate, argue, validate, decide.

Creativity, ask them to design, construct, revise, combine, compose, synthesize, produce, plan, develop, formulate.

MULTIPLE-CHOICE RESPONSES

Here's a MC example: What do we call the tough elastic tissues that connect bone to bone or support an organ?

a. tendons
b. muscles
c. ligaments
d. cartilage

As in the example, the main parts of a multiple choice item are the *stem*, which poses the question or problem, and the *options*, here labeled a, b, c, and d; they are the possible choices for the answer. One of the options is the correct response, called the *key*; the others are called *distracters*. A multiple-choice item may have two or more options. If only two options are offered, the item is essentially a true/false question. One sometimes finds in tests a multiple-choice item that intentionally has more than one correct option: they are the exception and must be flagged for student test-takers. Occasionally, even professional test writers inadvertently create an item with more than one correct response. These embarrassing errors are usually caught by an alert student test-taker.

Benefits of Multiple-Choice Items

1. Student response time is faster than for supply items like essays, or for performance assessments. So teachers can sample more important areas of the domains they are assessing, resulting in greater reliability and fairer scores for the students.
2. The time required for scoring an examination is greatly reduced. This feature facilitates rapid turnaround of exam results.
3. Scoring is more objective than for supply questions. In part, this benefit derives from the tendency of selection items to focus on verifiable facts and information, leaving little opportunity for nuances, or for incomplete or "creative" responses. Of course, that focus can also be considered a downside of selection responses.
4. Elsewhere in this book, we urge the value of item analysis. When a teacher has prepared a section of MC items with attractive, but not *too* attractive distracters, he can gain valuable insights into his students' thinking by reviewing the distracters, that is, the incorrect responses, his students chose.

Limitations of Multiple-Choice Items

1. The time one gains in grading can be lost in the preparation. Devising good multiple-choice items is often difficult. Sure, it's easy to posit an event and then give four possible dates for the responses. Except for relatively few significant dates, it's seems hard to justify requiring students to memorize the exact years in which events took place. Much the same holds for an English teacher giving an author's name, followed by the titles of four books, requiring students to choose which book the author wrote. But devising a question or problem on important course material, stating it concisely and clearly, preparing distracters that are reasonably plausible (three, plus the key are most common), ensuring that the key is correct and is the only correct response, avoiding giving away the key by making it differ from other options in length or grammar, all of these important guidelines can make constructing good multiple-choice items difficult.
2. In selection questions, the student doesn't create the answer, he recognizes it. That's by no means a shoddy way to solve a problem; for most problems in our daily lives, we don't start from scratch, we choose among various options or explanations. But in selecting an answer from a list in front of him, a student can guess. If he's not sure which option is correct, but recognizes that one or two of them are wrong, his odds improve. That doesn't mean the process is useless; again, in our

daily lives, certitude is often lacking. Making reasonable guesses is a useful ability. But on an exam, as in the rest of our lives, certitude is sometimes required and there may be a penalty for guessing wrong.

Preparing Multiple-Choice Items

1. Measure important learning outcomes, not stray facts that are easy to test but contribute little to students' learning.
2. State the problem (stem) as clearly and concisely as possible. Review and revise until you are sure that students can quickly read and understand what is being asked.
3. Usually, state the stem in a positive form. If you use a negative, highlight the negative term. "Which of the following is *not* . . ."
4. Be sure that the intended answer is the (only) correct one; that's not as obvious as it sounds. Review the items and, if possible, have a colleague do the same. If you intend that several possible responses are acceptable, or if you want students to choose the best answer among several plausible ones, be sure that students understand these variations. Especially with elementary grade children, it's better to stick with the usual MC format.
5. Make all options alike in terms of grammar and length. In an effort to ensure that the correct answer is absolutely, positively correct, teachers sometimes make the key longer than the other options. Bright kids catch on to this flaw in a nanosecond.
6. Use "all of the above," or "none of the above," sparingly. They are tempting when we want four options and are stuck after the third one. "All of the above" can be rejected by test-takers as soon as they recognize that even one option is incorrect. "None of the above" is less problematic, but it does allow students to respond simply by recognizing that the other options are wrong. Students cannot select the correct answer—a useful instructional activity—because it's not there. These limitations on "all" or "none" items simply suggest moderation in using them for classroom assessment.

Examples

Now let's consider how some of our recommendations and warnings are exemplified in MC items.

1. When did the following authors die?

   a. F. Scott Fitzgerald
   b. Homer
   c. Harriet Beecher Stowe
   d. Joyce Carol Oates

This is a really *bad* test item. Its flaws include: (1) It's trivia; who cares? The question does not assess knowledge that is important for students of literature. (2) As of this writing, Joyce Carol Oates is happily still among us. If intended as a trick question, it's as inappropriate as it is incorrect. (3) The options are not homogenous; Homer and Harriet Beecher Stowe differ enormously from one another and from the other two authors by period and genre. (4) What does "When" mean in the stem? An exact date? A century? Ancient versus modern times? Given all the possible worthwhile questions about these authors' contributions to literature, there is no excuse for so flawed and trivial a question.

2. A chemical bond is formed when electrons are

   a. gained
   b. lost
   c. shared
   d. all of the above

   One need not know much about chemical bonds to perceive that option d in extremely unlikely. A student who has never heard of chemical bonds now has a one in three chance of guessing the correct answer.

3. Evolution is a change in

   a. things as they grow older
   b. species over time
   c. characteristics of living things
   d. the history of the earth

   This is another bad question: (1) With just a little stretch, all of the options could be considered plausible. Options must be clearly defined from one another. (2) A vague word like "things" should not appear in a test question. (3) This is the kind of question that good students will waste time over, trying to figure out what the teacher is asking.

4. If $x-8 = 5y$ and $x = 23$, what is the value of $x-y$?

   a. 3
   b. 10
   c. 15
   d. 20

   This is a legitimate item, requiring students to create a simple equation and solve for y. This is also a two-step problem; students should be reminded to read each stem carefully. In this case they are not asked for the value of y, but for $x-y$.

MATCHING ITEMS

In matching items, as in multiple-choice items, the correct response lies in front of the test-taker. A teacher prepares a column of some ten names, events, or something similar and a second, slightly longer column of time periods, geographical locations, events, titles, and such. The student's task is to match each entry in the first column with an entry in the second column. Even more than multiple-choice items, these matching questions focus on lower-level but important cognitive skills. So, matching items are an efficient way to examine students' familiarity with a great deal of information. Forgive us for saying, one more time, that testing for information is a legitimate and even indispensable classroom exercise; in every subject, there is a lot we must commit to memory. But results of matching and MC items should be enriched with students' responses to more complex item types.

Benefits of Matching Items

1. Critics rightly complain of recognitions items that have no context, they are unrelated to what students have learned or will learn. At their best, matching items ask students to perceive important relationships; for younger students especially, this skill is an important element in their gaining basic thinking skills and cultural literacy. When we want students to place people or events in time periods or geographical locations, when we test their ability to relate examples to principles or rules, matching items are an efficient technique to gather a great deal of information in a single item.

2. Students often enjoy matching questions, seeing the terms as pieces of a puzzle they are to assemble. The task is clear and students can move quickly through a matching item if the choices in column B are reasonably discrete. If, for example, a world history teacher wants to place a list of events in column A within their time periods, she could make the periods in column B in centuries, rather than specific years.

3. A matching item is relatively easy to prepare and yields multiple scores. Student response time is usually short, although papers of less well-informed students may have a number of erasures, as these students are lured into responding too quickly by a plausible match, only to find a better one in reading further in column B.

4. Scoring a matching item is quick and simple. That benefit assumes that, in preparing the question, a teacher has carefully ensured that each item in column A has a correct match in column B. In fact, a teacher may choose to have one response serve more than one question. That variation must, of course, be made clear to students.

Limitations of Matching Items

1. The information gained from matching items is factual in nature. Specifically, the correct answers show how one item in the first column relates to one in the second column.
2. If students make an incorrect match in the first few pairings, they can be delayed as they search for a correct match for a later question because the correct response is already taken. If a student gets one match wrong, he will almost certainly make another error. A teacher may, however, want a response in column B to serve two items in column A.
3. Matching items are a variation of multiple-choice; they present not four options, but ten or more. Less able students can become confused by having to read and choose among ten fairly plausible answers.

Preparing Matching Items

1. As always, begin by asking, "Why am I asking these questions? What knowledge or skill do I want my students to demonstrate?" If the answer is "analysis," or "critical thinking," choose another item type.
2. Are the "matches" in column B homogeneous? That is, are they all people, or places, periods, and the like? A mix of responses can be confusing as to the nature of the relationship or conversely, can clue test-takers to the desired match.
3. Do I have more responses in column B than questions in column A? The same number of items in both columns will tip off test-takers, especially for the final few items.
4. Have I carefully edited my matching items to make the entries in both columns as succinct as possible? This important step eliminates clues and reduces students' reading time.
5. Do I intend and state that each response may be used only once, or more than once?
6. Is the entire matching item with its directions contained on a single page?

SUMMARY

- The chapter first defines the relative merits of various types of assessment, and explains how to choose the item type that best demonstrates certain skills and knowledge taught in a classroom.
- An example of a multiple-choice item shows the characteristics of the item type. That explanation is followed by sections on the benefits and limitations of multiple-choice questions. Several examples illustrate the steps teachers follow in preparing multiple-choice items.
- Matching items share many of the advantages and disadvantages of multiple-choice items. They can show students' understanding of context and relationships, but are largely limited to demonstrating recall and comprehension. Matching questions have certain specific requirements for their preparation.

5

Supply Responses

When students are asked to supply responses to questions or problems, they are faced with a different and, arguably, more difficult task than is required for recognition items. As the word *supply* suggests, students cannot search for the answer in an array of options in front of them, but must construct—supply—the correct responses. Among traditional item types, supply items cover the widest range of cognitive skills, from remembering a single word on a fill-in-the-blank item to the highest levels of evaluation and creativity in a term paper or an extended essay question.

How do teachers choose the types of items that are most efficient and appropriate? The golden rule is, first, decide on the knowledge and skills that students should display on the test: Definitions and comprehension? Recall of facts or principles? Comprehension? Application? Analysis? Synthesis? Evaluation and judgment? (See chapter 4 for verbs that call for these skills.) Choose the type of item that most effectively and efficiently demonstrates the desired skills.

Before we consider specific types of supply items, let's review a few general principles that can guide teachers as they plan for an upcoming exam, using various kinds of supply items.

First, the golden rule: Decide what knowledge and skills students should demonstrate on the test.

Second, adjust the choice of item types to the abilities and needs of the student test-takers. Items that require reading, such as a critical reading passage, or considerable writing, such as an extended essay on a timed examination, pose greater obstacles for many special education students or those for whom English is a second language than do items requiring shorter responses.

Third, provide clear directions and a focused statement of the task; especially for extended essay questions, use terms that encourage students to analyze, evaluate, and synthesize, and to respond creatively. Setting boundaries is important for extended essays, but even more critical for restricted essays. This principle may sound counterintuitive for encouraging creative or alternative thinking, but vague directions can lead to meandering responses that pose problems when teachers score the answers.

Fourth, remember the basic principles of validity and reliability. Other things being equal, an examination that includes many well-crafted items can enhance both of those qualities because students have more opportunities to display what they know. Essay exams are powerful tools for applying higher-order thinking, and a well-designed essay can yield scores on several important elements of a course. But a major examination that relies on scores from one or a few essays cannot cover all or even most of the significant learning in a course; using an essay to cover the objectives for an entire course raises doubts about the reliability and validity of any grade derived from that examination.

Now, let's look at the descriptions of supply items and the knowledge and skills they measure.

FILL IN THE BLANK

Ms. Lovesey is giving her third graders a test on a story read in class. She included the following item: "The hero of the story was _____." Most of the class wrote "Sweetie," the name of the dog who was the hero of the story. One of her students, Peter, wrote, "a dog."

Ms. Lovesey first marks the latter answer wrong, reasoning that the other students understood what was asking and answered correctly. Then she considered that Peter's response was, in fact, correct. Of course, Peter should get credit for his response; it's Ms. Lovesey who gets a low grade for preparing an item that has more than one correct answer.

The fill-in-the-blank item type has much in common with the multiple-choice format in its brevity, ease of scoring, and the level of cognitive skills it probes. It appears deceptively easy to construct; some teachers simply look for a declarative statement in a text and copy it on to a test, with one keyword blank. If the statement is an important one for the purposes of the course, such an easily constructed item is satisfactory.

When students are told to fill in the blank, they may come up with responses their teacher didn't anticipate. Teachers should be willing to accept plausible substitutes for their intended answers. But such an item is confusing, especially for well-informed students, as they perceive more than one correct answer when only one is called for. It is essential, as teachers prepare the test, that they carefully review the wording of their questions so as to avoid ambiguity.

What are the pros and cons of using fill-in items in a classroom test?

Fill in the blank is a *good* technique for measuring basic information with a somewhat more challenging requirement than is true of recognition items; the method can be employed to measure basic comprehension, such as recognition and identification, or problem solving without showing process.

Fill-in items are a *fair* way to measure a student's ability to explain and describe.

Fill-in items are *poor* at allowing students to demonstrate cognitive skills beyond comprehension.

In preparing fill-in items, we recommend that teachers:

1. Use a complete question or statement.
2. Do not use questions that lend themselves to several plausible responses.
3. Be willing to accept an unanticipated, but acceptable alternative response.
4. Place the blank at the end of the sentence whenever possible.
5. Use sentences/paragraphs with multiple blanks sparingly. Such questions are very challenging for some students, especially those with reading problems.
6. Avoid trivia. Even at this basic level of test item, devise questions that test facts or comprehension that are important elements in the subject.

SHORT-ANSWER QUESTIONS

Mr. Tanenbaum presents the following question to his U.S. Government class: The First Amendment of the U.S. Constitution bars Congress from making certain laws. What laws does the First Amendment forbid Congress to enact?

In this question we see some similarities to the fill-in items described previously, but the item requires a lengthier and more complex response. Short-answer questions look primarily for knowledge and comprehension, but may demand responses with several phrases or sentences; they may sometimes be used for assessing more complex skills. Often they lend themselves to partial credit. In this example we see how this is possible. A student whose response reads, "Laws that interfere with religion and with freedom of speech" certainly deserves substantial credit; one who enumerated the six provisos of the amendment should receive more points.

Note that this item could easily be translated into a multiple-choice stem with numerous options, including "all of the above." Or it could become a matching item. Either of those formats would make it an easier item, because it's more difficult to remember and enumerate the provisos of the First Amendment than it is to recognize them.

Let's consider what short-answer items are *good* for:

1. This item type can be use to demonstrate basic knowledge, ranging from straightforward recall of information to definition of rules and principles.
2. Short answers can be used to classify, describe, and explain.
3. They can also call for brief application responses; these may consist of a written demonstration, an illustration, an outline, or a brief description of a process.

Short-answer items are *fair* for:

1. Analysis—when a brief critique, or a brief comparison/contrast, is called for.
2. Application—when students are asked to move from a general principle or example to specific statements or descriptions.

Short-answers are *poor* for:

1. Complex analysis that may be required in explaining a laboratory experiment or a work of literature.
2. Evaluation and design, as when outcomes or objectives must be appraised or a thesis constructed.

In preparing and scoring short-answer problems, we recommend considering these key points:

1. The practices for preparing short answer items parallel those for fill-in-the-blank questions, but the wording of short answers requires extra care to avoid ambiguities and to direct students toward the desired responses.
2. Even when the first recommendation is observed, the potential for unexpected but acceptable responses to the one intended is increased. The same holds for partially correct answers, which are common with short-answer questions.

3. With short-answer responses, the issue of reader reliability arises; reliability becomes a pressing concern as we explore more complex types of
supply items. The focus in scoring short-answer items must be on the
content of the response, not on the students who provide them ("Sarah
is such a good student, I'm sure what she meant to say was . . ."). Nor
should a scorer consider extraneous elements like neatness or spelling
(unless it's a spelling test).

ESSAYS

Our explanation of supply items moves from the simple to the complex:
from filling in a blank to the greater effort and potential of short-answer
items, and now to restricted and extended essays. We begin with a few general remarks about essays as assessment.

First, recall from chapter 2 our insistence that, as teachers, we should always ask, "What can students learn from our assessments?" The more complex the form of assessment, the greater the possibility that student learning
can occur. Essays, and performance assessment (the topic of the next chapter), should probe complex skills, especially analysis and critical thinking.
These item types are potentially the best form of assessment because students can gain important knowledge and skills in the process of responding.

Second, be sure that essay questions do what they do best, that is, give students an opportunity to display higher-order cognitive skills. This places a responsibility on the teacher to choose topics that call for these skills, to word
the topic carefully, and to provide full directions. "Full directions" means
clear instructions on *what* students are expected to do, *how* they are to do it,
and how much *time* they will have in class, or a due date for a paper.

Third, essays make greater demands on students' understanding and concentration than simpler types of assessment. Students are more likely to respond as best as they possibly can if, in a period prior to the exam, their
teachers prepare them by explaining and giving examples of good essays.
Anything teachers can do to minimize distractions and keep students focused on their task will also help the quality of the assessment and the validity of the responses.

Fourth, scoring essays is almost as much an art as writing them. The choice
of scoring method—holistic, analytic, or a combination of the two—affects the
precision and usefulness of the scores and the time required to grade the essays. One author (Gronlund, 2006, p. 115) refers to the scoring of essays as,
"Subjective, difficult, and less reliable than recognition items." We'll describe
and suggest choices among essay-scoring protocols as we consider each type

of essay. Meanwhile, don't be discouraged. The potential richness of students' responses means that essays really are worth the trouble!

But first, let's consider another hazard of essay scoring: the "halo effect." This is the tendency to give more credit to a student known to be a capable writer, or whose previous answers on the exam are very good. Keeping essay writers anonymous during the scoring is one way to combat the halo effect. If an exam has multiple essays, a teacher can reduce the influence of prior answers by scoring the first essay response on every student's paper, then scoring the second response, and so on. For a major examination, ask a colleague to grade at least some papers and compare the results with your own. By moderating the halo effect, teaches reduce systematic bias in their scoring and increase the reliability of the scoring process.

Now let's examine in more detail the use of restricted and extended essays for assessment.

Restricted Essays

As the title suggests, restricted essays are less free-ranging than their extended counterparts. With restricted essays, teachers constrain and focus students' responses by giving explicit directions on what and how they should address the essay topic.

Ms. Morse is preparing the semester exam for her English literature students. For a restricted essay question she chose this item:

> William Wordsworth is described as a giant of English poetry, but one whose poetry has many imperfections. What are Wordsworth's greatest strengths as a poet? What are his imperfections? Your response should be in one or two paragraphs, no more than half a page; you should take about ten minutes to answer the questions.

Let's assume that Ms. Morse has taught Wordsworth and his works and has coached her class on writing restricted essays. The questions proposed in the item ask students to describe specific qualities attributed to a poet; in responding, students will explain, interpret, and summarize—all action words that characterize a restricted essay item. If Ms. Morse were proposing an extended essay with fewer restrictions and more available response time, she might ask her students to give examples from Wordsworth's poetry of his literary strengths and weaknesses, or to compare and contrast him with another poet.

Preparing Restricted Essay Items

1. Start with our golden rule: Ask, "What do I want my students to learn in preparing for, responding to, and reviewing the results of this question?"

2. Tell students they should carefully restrict their responses to the specific questions posed in the item. Urge them to focus narrowly on what they are asked to do: describe, propose, list, summarize?

3. Define the appropriate length of responses and the time available for them. The time restraints that characterize both restricted and extended essay questions on in-class exams raise concerns about some students' responses, as some students write slowly and feel pressured and distracted by time limits. This time constraint is also a basis for questioning the validity of tests of "writing skills" in the very limited time allotted for the essay portion of most standardized examinations.

4. Review the questions and the model responses with a colleague, if possible.

5. Consider giving students a choice of topics. Most measurement experts discourage creating several different exams by giving students a choice of topics for essays. But we suggest that what is lost in comparing students with one another is compensated for by giving students an opportunity to provide their best performance. Either "choice" or "no choice" seems justifiable.

Scoring Restricted Essays

1. Analytic scoring is the most effective approach for restricted essays. A good rule of thumb for analytic scoring is to choose four to six important elements that should appear in a response, assign a range of point values to each element (for example, one to five), then read a student's response and total the points awarded. Note that, unlike other disciplines, English language or literature exams may properly be scored on grammar and spelling.

2. The scoring of restricted essays, like their preparation, should reflect the knowledge and skills taught in the course. If, in her English literature class, Ms. Morse instructed her students in close reading and analysis of texts, we would expect her essay questions to be scored on students' use of analysis, interpretation, and the ability to draw inferences.

3. Prepare a model response. This scoring guide prepared by the classroom teacher for her restricted essay items should also be tightly constrained. It should set a very limited number of criteria on which each question will be scored, always allowing for the occasional, unexpected insight on a student's part. We recommend setting explicit, limited scoring criteria in part to aid teachers' efficiency in grading papers. In addition, focusing on a few key elements can improve the reliability of the scores and grades.

Benefits and Limitations of Restricted Essays

On one hand:

1. Students can demonstrate their ability to go beyond recalling information; restricted essays are a good means of showing comprehension, application, and analysis.
2. The format allows students some freedom in responding, while focusing them on key elements of the responses.
3. The use of an analytical scoring guide allows teachers to score and grade restricted essays fairly rapidly.

On the other hand:

1. In a class period, only a few restricted essay questions can be presented. Requiring only a few items limits the breadth of content coverage. For a major exam, use other items as well.
2. Even with careful preparation of scoring protocols, some subjectivity will creep into the scoring process, further reducing the reliability of results.

We believe that the bottom line is to use restricted essays whenever time permits. They are an excellent means of focusing both teachers and students on important content and skills taught in a course. In an exam that intends to cover a great deal of course content, for example, a semester or final exam, restricted essays should be supplemented by briefer items that more broadly sample the material in the course.

Extended Essays: An Example

Extended essays could be termed the "gold standard" of classroom and standardized testing. They allow students the maximum opportunity to display their most complex cognitive skills and to organize their responses in a coherent and convincing fashion. These are skills that are difficult or impossible to display through other assessment procedures.

Ms. Peters has prepared a final exam for her European history class. She is administering the assessment over two class periods: one day's exam has many items, primarily recognition and short-answer-type questions, with the second day reserved for a single essay question. In several periods in advance of the examination, Ms. Peters reviewed the major elements studied in the course, explained the types of questions on the exam, and discussed with the class the most efficient and effective ways to respond to the various item types, with special emphasis on the qualities of a good essay. On the second day of the final, Ms. Peters told her students that they had 50 minutes to write the essay, and she would remind them when 10 minutes' time remained. Her essay question read:

Why was Great Britain so dominant a power during the nineteenth century? Analyze and evaluate the effects of three factors that led to Britain's prominence. Then compare Britain's achievements with those of France during the same period; why did France not achieve the same level of dominance as England?

(Note that Ms. Peters could have made the question easier for her students by listing several factors in the question, or by eliminating the comparison with nineteenth-century France.)

In her references to analysis and evaluation, as well as comparisons and explanations, Ms. Peters's question demonstrates important qualities of an extended essay item.

1. Information and comprehension: Yes, students first need to know and understand many facts about nineteenth-century England and France—the industrial revolution, the rise of nationalism, the revolutions of 1848, population growth in the two countries, and so on—if they are to respond properly.
2. Organization: Students are not simply to compile lists, but are to weave the factors into a coherent essay, showing cause and effect.
3. Critical judgment and creative thinking: An extended essay gives an opportunity to exercise these skills. Evaluation and creative thought rely not on vaguely supported attitudes and opinions, but are developed out of the understanding and interpretation of learning that the students have gained in class and by study outside of class.

An extended essay, then, is a student's response to a carefully crafted question or set of questions that call for the exercise of many levels of cognitive skills, including the most complex.

Teachers who use extended essays soon come to recognize two types of student who occasionally surface in essay writing. We call them the "stuffers" and the "clutchers." The stuffer believes that more is better, so his essay is a lengthy response crammed with factual data that is more or less relevant to the topic. The result is a list of facts rather than an organized set of information woven into an engaging essay. On a timed test, the stuffer usually sacrifices the important elements of essay style and the connection of information for breadth of information and heavy detail. The clutcher writes and writes, often producing a fine introduction and early elements of a good response, but she runs out of time. She's the one who clutches her paper and appeals for "just another minute." In reading the clutcher's paper, a teacher may see a strong introduction, a body on its way to development, then a hastily scrawled finish to the body, and no conclusion. Teachers can warn incipient stuffers and clutchers of the probable results of their response styles, but these habits are hard to break. We recommend providing students with "low risk" opportunities for improvement by assigning timed practice essays. These practice runs can materially assist students when they face essay questions in standardized exams; they also provide opportunities for peer review in a classroom. If these clutching and stuffing tendencies can be overcome through practice in your classroom, you will have done students a favor they will appreciate for years to come.

Preparing an Extended Essay Item

Scoring extended essays can be a challenge for teachers, but devising good essay questions is not so easy either. Clarifying the skills that students are expected to display is obviously critical, but so are the preparation for the exam and the directions that immediately precede the administration. We recommend the following steps in preparing essay questions:

1. Ask "What do we want students to learn from this exam? From this question?" That familiar query is most appropriate when we compose an essay question. In our previous example, Ms. Peters hopes that her students are reminded of and will reflect on significant political and economic elements in two nineteenth-century nations. She will touch on these factors in her review prior to the examination and will discuss the responses with the class after the exam.
2. Minimize verbs that call for straightforward recall of factual information concerning terminology or details. The process of the response, specifically the words teachers use in stating the question, is the vital element. Ask students to interpret, infer, give examples, plan, organize, judge, generate, construct. Of course, students must have learned how to interpret, infer, and so on.
3. Review the major knowledge and skills taught in the course, and don't hesitate to hint that several of these will appear as topics or requirements in the final exam. Remember: We want our students to learn the most important elements of our courses and we want them to do well on the exams.
4. Give clear directions for student responses before the essay questions are distributed. In part, this requirement is covered in periods prior to the exam. But on exam day, a teacher should read aloud the essay question and the directions that should also be printed on the examination paper. The response time available, the allocation of points that will be credited for each item (if there are several of them), any restrictions on

length of answers, and a reminder to *please* write legibly are all appropriate. Questions may be permitted before the exam begins.

5. When the teacher's scoring guide (see Scoring Extended Essays, which follows) includes the important knowledge and principal skills the teacher calls for in the question, the preparation of the guide can help to improve the wording of the question.

Scoring Extended Essays

For restricted essays we have recommended that teachers use *analytic* scoring. In this approach, each criterion of a response is scored separately. *Holistic* scoring is a process often used with extended essays and performance measures. A scoring guide lists the principal criteria on which the essay or performance will be judged. A teacher then rapidly reviews the product of the assessment and assigns a grade that represents a total, general impression of quality. A four-point scale works best; it does not make unreliably fine distinctions and avoids the equivocating middle ground of a three on a five-point scale. Holding the scale to a few points also avoids the twofold difficulty derived from a scale of eight or more points. That is, first, the objective of greater exactness is an illusion, as holistic scoring does not lend itself to precision, and scores become less reliable. Second, the more scale points, the greater the time spent in the scoring of each paper.

For all our positive feelings about essay questions, we must note two cautions. One problem, mentioned earlier, is the limited reliability of scores based on a single or a few test items. Note that our Ms. Peters works around that problem by giving one exam with many items, followed by a single essay exam, then weighting the respective scores, and merging them into a single grade. This model, used in most Advanced Placement examinations, has much to recommend it. The second concern about using essay measures is the point of this section: Scoring tends to be subjective, thus less reliable than for more objective items. So, what can teachers do to enhance the reliability of essay scores?

1. Scoring really begins with the preparation of the essay question. A question that communicates to students the knowledge and skills they are to employ and gives them clear directions enhances the reliability of scoring.
2. Prepare a model answer (scoring guide) that matches each element of the question. The effort devoted to preparing a model response can greatly improve the efficiency of the scoring process.
3. Reliability can be improved if a teacher scores each student's paper anonymously. If there are several essay questions, score the first one on all papers before moving to the second question, and so on. Both

recommendations are intended to reduce the "halo effect," the possibility of being influenced by factors other than the quality of response itself.

4. For each major criterion in the scoring guide, set a point value. In Ms. Peters's example, she would consider students' judgments on the impact of political changes, and/or economic developments in Britain and France as important criteria for appraising the responses. We suggest using no more than four to five elements and a corresponding number of points for each criterion.

5. If at all possible, have a colleague review the essay questions, the scoring guide, and a sample of scored papers. When a colleague's grade differs significantly from our own, we are reminded of the reliability issue in essay exams; we should also be encouraged to use multiple assessments in determining student grades.

6. Don't let the quantity of a response substitute for quality. We have observed in essay scores on some standardized tests that the longer the answer, the higher the grade. Writers should not be rewarded for wordiness that fills up a page without addressing the required knowledge and skills.

7. Teachers should, however, be willing to accept unanticipated answers that appropriately address the question. Remember that essays should permit students to display creativity and other complex skills.

Benefits and Limitations of Extended Essays

Extended essays are an important part of a teacher's assessment strategies, and we've indicated some of the benefits and drawbacks of this item type. In brief:

1. Well-prepared essay questions are an excellent way to probe for higher-order learning skills. However, they are an inefficient means of measuring more basic elements of learning, such as recognizing or recalling factual knowledge.

2. In preparing for and writing essay questions, students are developing important elements of their writing skills, quite apart from the content of their responses.

3. The limitations of essay questions focus on the reliability of the scores: Only a few questions can be posed within a limited time for assessment and, in scoring essays, teachers are hard put to avoid all subjectivity.

4. The benefits from analytic and holistic scoring differ. When students receive a paper that their teacher has scored analytically, they gain useful information about the strengths and weakness of their responses.

A single holistic grade can invite questions from students (and parents). On the other hand, experienced teachers can make judgments that are more than the sum of their parts. But let's be frank; a great advantage of holistic scoring is that it makes far fewer demands on teachers' time and energies than do analytically scored measures. That's a perfectly defensible benefit.

SUMMARY

- Supply items require students to create, not simply to recognize a response; they can cover the widest range of cognitive skills.
- Supply items include fill-in-the-blank and short-answer responses, but they best tap higher-order skills through restricted and extended essays.
- Before considering individual item types, the text provides some general guidelines for all supply-type items. Fill-in and short-answer items are reviewed, with explanations and examples of their preparation, scoring, and merits.
- The greater part of the chapter concerns essay items. They are recommended for their ability to assess higher-order skills, but are efficient only for those purposes, not for measuring more basic knowledge and skills.
- Scoring, especially for extended essays, is time-consuming and less exact than is true for other kinds of items.
- This chapter includes directions for preparing and scoring restricted and extended essays, and speaks to the benefits and limitations of those item types.

6

Authentic and Performance Assessment

REALISTIC ASSESSMENT

If extended essays are the gold standard of written assessment, authentic/performance assessment may be termed the diamond or platinum standard. The strongest evidence of knowledge or skills is found in their actual use. An example is the various tests for obtaining a first driver's license. Candidates must pass a written test of their knowledge of road rules, followed by a vision test. Both are reasonable requirements for determining whether an individual is prepared to drive. Then comes the performance test; a novice driver is observed and rated by a driving inspector while the candidate drives under various road conditions.

On a written physics exam, students can describe the conditions and procedures to conduct an experiment in weightlessness. When the students then conduct such an experiment, the written knowledge and skills they described become a reality test; to what extent does the experiment prove that students understand and can apply their knowledge? That assessment becomes a still more useful instructional experience by having students write a lab report, explaining the results of the experiment in relation to the principles and rules it demonstrates.

Performance assessment simply means carrying out a task that demonstrates knowledge and skills in an observable way. *Authentic* assessment is produced under naturalistic conditions, that is, with minimal contextual constraints. It is sometimes used as a synonym for performance assessment but it can also mean a more complex task. Students not only create a product, they may also plan and organize all elements of the task, including how the outcomes can be evaluated.

Both performance and authentic assessment focus on real-life tasks that require learners to demonstrate specific knowledge and skills. One could argue that virtually all assessment or student achievement is "performance," that is, students must do something—write, recite, ask, respond to questions—that enables a teacher to perceive the extent of learning that has taken place. When we link performance and authentic assessment, as in this chapter, we are speaking of both basic and more complex performance that applies and replicates as closely as possible the skills being measured.

Another example: A grasp of vocabulary and rules of grammar are certainly reasonable elements on which Madame Poirot can test her second-year French class. A one-page essay to be written in French, or a two-minute oral presentation will demonstrate students' ability to apply their skills in the language. The intended outcomes are performances: The best evidence that students have learned to read, write, speak, and listen is when they demonstrate those skills.

One more example of performance assessment is the Milestone requirement at Princeton (New Jersey) Charter School. In each grade, students are assigned two academic projects to be completed over the course of a semester or school year, one of which must be in a language arts or quantitative area. The purposes of the projects are to focus the curriculum, emphasize and give evidence of key skills, and honor students' achievement. Classroom teachers mentor the projects and provide interim feedback, but the final products or performances are evaluated by another teacher or an external rater. Students who successfully complete their projects receive certificates at an annual assembly. The projects include keyboarding skills and physical education performances, as well as conducting and writing up a laboratory experiment, writing and performing a skit in Spanish or French, and tasks in the areas of reading, writing, and mathematics.

We strongly favor performance assessment whenever it is feasible. But in addressing issues of preparing and scoring performance assessment we point out the importance of the phrase "whenever . . . feasible." In this chapter, we examine feasibility and other issues related to preparing and scoring performance items. We also discuss how well performance assessment satisfies the three major qualities of good assessment: validity, reliability, and efficiency.

PREPARING PERFORMANCE ITEMS

Performance testing has much in common with essay assessment, including possibilities for brief or restricted performances, and lengthier, more complex activities. The preparation and advantages of each type correspond with their characteristics: A restricted performance item can be stated briefly and performed quickly, with a sharply focused task and simple scoring rubrics. An extended performance task, like the longer essay, requires more careful preparation, and a task that encourages maximum student independence and initiative; scoring is more difficult and less precise. We suggest the following directions for preparing both restricted and extended performance items:

1. Begin with our favorite question: What do we want students to learn from this assessment? That query is especially appropriate for performance tests, because they require practice—actually doing what is to be learned. That excellent characteristic of performance assessment is especially prominent in the arts. A music teacher instructs her students, then listens and evaluates as they perform a work. An art teacher explains and shows examples of watercolors, then observes how students carry out his instructions for creating watercolors and notes the quality of the finished product. Learning is applied and exemplified in the students' performance. The same holds for physical education; students' ability to throw a ball or skate, do pushups or run a mile can only be assessed through observing and rating their performance in those skills.

2. Keep in mind that performance assessment is best used to probe students' skills in applying, constructing, demonstrating, organizing, and creating. For basic cognitive skills like recalling or comprehending, recognition items are more efficient.

3. Determine whether a *process* or a *product* is the primary objective of the assessment. Some performance assessment is principally intended to yield a summative judgment: pass/fail or A–F. Because the product results from an actual demonstration of the desired knowledge and skills, one can draw inferences about the quality of the process. When students are asked to create a sculpture for art class, their teacher can examine the product, perhaps at various stages of execution, and determine whether appropriate processes have been followed. For many performance assessments, for example, those that emphasize oral or physical skills, the process that is observed becomes, in effect, a product of the assessment. When a math teacher tells her students to "show all your work," she is looking for process, how the students reached an answer. But generally, a product is preferable to a process, as it is more efficient and more reliable to assess.

4. State the overall purpose of the performance assessment. Using another example, Ms. Diaz says, "I want to determine the conversational ability of my fourth-year Spanish students."

5. Given that overall purpose, Ms. Diaz then lists the principal criteria by which she will judge her students' conversational skills: use of complex

sentences, an extensive, correctly used vocabulary, accent, fluency, and evidence of comprehension.

6. Ms. Diaz then carefully plans the performance task (a process in which students converse in Spanish) to satisfy the purpose and exemplify the skills that she seeks to assess. So, our teacher designates pairs of students who will converse in front of their classmates, and then gives them their topics and perhaps a starter question or sentences. She also designates a length of time for their conversations and may give each pair a few minutes' preparation time. Ms. Diaz devises a simple checklist that she uses to rate her students' performance. As she observes each student's conversation, for every criterion she checks a number on a four-point scale—with one signifying Minimal Skills and four equaling Excellent. She may also ask her students to rate their own and each others' performances.

SCORING PERFORMANCE ITEMS

The scoring of performance assessments can be a challenge to reliability if the rating criteria are not clearly defined. The problem is especially acute in scoring a process, which is transitory, thus more difficult to observe and rate than a product.

Note, too, that some performances require cooperative efforts on the part of several participants. The star center on a basketball team will probably not score many points if the guards don't get the ball to him. The same holds for musicians in an orchestra. A violinist's masterful performance may be lost amid the flaws of fellow performers. Scoring and evaluating each individual's performance or contribution to the performance is difficult when a project involves a group effort.

Usually, individuals' contributions begin to emerge when there are multiple opportunities to rate the process, or when several products are created. We believe that the learning derived from students sharing the responsibility and effort on an occasional project more than counterbalances the inevitable imprecision of assigning individual credit. It may be fair simply to assign the same grade on the project to all members of a group. Simply be sure that other means of assessing individuals are employed.

We make these suggestions for meeting challenges to scoring performances:

1. Remember our cautions about using a single assessment to make a global judgment. Whenever possible, replicate and reassess the task, especially if what is being scored is a process. Supplement the performance assessment with results from other forms of assessment be-

fore assigning a final grade or deciding who makes the varsity team, for instance.

2. Begin a performance scoring guide by stating the overall purpose and the most important criteria in the process.
3. Break each major quality or criterion into a four-point scale; for each point on the scale, prepare a brief description of the qualities or evidence that correspond with the scale point.
4. Ensure that student participants are informed and reminded of the elements on which they will be judged. Warn them about distractions or the inclusion of trivial elements.
5. Further the instructional benefit by building in a self/group evaluation process.
6. Be open to alternative, creative responses.

BENEFITS AND LIMITATIONS OF PERFORMANCE ASSESSMENTS

The benefits of using performance measures are these:

1. This mode of assessment could also be termed "performance instruction"; more opportunities for learning result from performance measures than from other forms of assessment. When students practice what they have been taught by planning and creating, by carrying out a process or devising a product, they learn more and better than by reading or listening.
2. Performance assessment provides direct evidence of competence; it does not use the proxy or intermediate step of describing orally or in writing how to do something, but gives immediate evidence of ability.
3. With performance appraisal, teachers can test all requirements of a task, from the basic to the most complex.
4. Performance is intrinsically interesting, thus more motivating to students than the typical paper and pencil test. "Book learning" can come alive when it is applied in a performance.
5. It is a highly valid form of assessment. When students actually *do* something, their performance is convincing evidence that they *can* do it.

The limitations of performance assessment include:

1. It is time-consuming to organize and carry out most performance assessments. When the task is to measure the performance of an entire group, the time is probably well spent; when individual competence

is to be measured, performance situations are more problematic. So, performance measures can be termed efficient for group assessment, but less efficient in most instances for assessing individuals. Note, however, that when an individual assessment leads to an important outcome, for example, a driver's license or the lead role in a school play, the time required is usually justified.

2. When an assessment of an individual takes place within a group performance, such as a football scrimmage or an orchestra rehearsal, the individual's score may not be very reliable.

3. Reliability is a general problem with performance measures. We know that the performance of an individual or a group varies from one performance to another. The golfer who cards a 78 today may score 90 a few days later. When a score is determined by an observer, an additional element affects reliability. Even using a carefully designed rating form, an observer's application of the criteria may, for several reasons, vary from one evaluation to another, or between individuals who are observed. Scoring protocols used in many Olympic sports are examples of attempts to improve reliability by using trained judges who employ carefully designed criteria, and by requiring several examples of an individual's performance, for example, a diver's or a skater's skills.

PORTFOLIO ASSESSMENT

Portfolios are organized collections of students' work. They are often intended to show development of skills over time, but they may also be collections only of students' best work. Portfolios are frequently used in writing classes; for developmental purposes, they may include outlines, drafts, revisions, and final products, as well as teachers' comments and students' own evaluations and reflections on their writing. Portfolios are also commonly used in the arts and in science classes.

An early and excellent example of portfolio assessment in the arts was the Arts PROPEL project, in which researchers from Harvard University and Educational Testing Service joined with Pittsburgh's Public School System (Harvard University School of Education, 2007). Portfolios were prepared by students in music, imaginative writing, and visual arts. The approach focused on three central aspects of the artistic process: production, perception, and reflection. The project was both process and product oriented: Along with their best work, students included drafts and research notes and recorded their thoughts and perceptions during the process.

Designing a Portfolio Assessment

If students are to gain maximum benefit from compiling a portfolio of their work, their teachers should first consider the following points:

1. Naturally, our first question is, "What do I want my students to learn from this project?" Because portfolios compile the students' own work over a period of time, they are, potentially, excellent instructional tools. The extent and quality of that instruction depend heavily on a teacher's careful definition of the purpose of the portfolio and the knowledge and skills he wants his student to learn through a portfolio assignment.
2. The next step is to decide what examples of students' work will best serve the portfolio's purpose. In his science class, Mr. Hill wants his students to reflect on and integrate the knowledge and skills they gain from their texts, lectures, discussions, and labs. He intends the assessment to be a creative learning opportunity for his students, so the portfolios are to include students' reflections on scientific discoveries, critiques of hypotheses, and descriptions of scientific phenomena, as well as models of scientific systems and plans for laboratory experiments. Mr. Hill provides guidelines and examples to help students choose and comment on their entries.
3. For each major entry, Mr. Hill encourages his students to reflect on what they learned and how they can apply that learning. If they are describing an experiment or criticizing a hypothesis or theory, they should say how they would improve it. Again, the learning is primary; the assessment becomes a vehicle for that learning.
4. Portfolios can be compiled over a school year, a semester, or a single grading period. As with any lengthy project, teachers should schedule interim reviews of the work in progress, providing feedback to encourage and/or correct the process. These periodic checkups can form a practical basis for student-teacher or parent-teacher conferences.

Scoring Portfolio Assessments

1. For a classroom portfolio project, we suggest that when a student has followed directions and conscientiously maintained a portfolio over several months the grade on the final product should range from satisfactory to excellent. That concession sounds like a violation of our earlier ban on using "effort" in grading academic achievement. In assembling a portfolio, the effort is part of the process bring evaluated. The reflections it contains may not be profound, or the plans complex

(although such enrichment would be laudable). In a well-designed and monitored assessment, almost every student's portfolio offers evidence of growth in learning.

2. However, when a local or state school system uses portfolio assessment for summative purposes, or if the portfolio is the sole element in a student's grade, it should be scored and graded more rigorously. Some states have mandated portfolio assessment, alone or with other data, as the basis for decisions about schools as well as students.

3. The great problem with ascribing a specific score to a portfolio, and in using that score for summative judgments, is the often demonstrated reality that an equally qualified grader might give that portfolio a very different score; in other words, reliability in scoring portfolios tends to range from moderate to poor. A score of doubtful reliability is not a fair or valid basis for major decisions about a student, an entire grade, or a school.

4. Scoring a portfolio is not a one-time event. Much of the learning in compiling portfolios comes from the back and forth, student to teacher to student interaction over the course of a portfolio project. Teachers who use portfolios in their classes have to accept the time-consuming task of periodically reviewing each student's progress and offering comments, guidance for additional resources, and so on.

Benefits and Limitations of Portfolios

Among the benefits of using portfolios for assessment are the following:

1. They can clarify standards for learning, as students apply them to the selection of their work.
2. They encourage students to feel responsible for the quality of their work.
3. They assist students in becoming more analytical.
4. Students are, in effect, competing with themselves, not their classmates.
5. The great benefit of a carefully planned portfolio assessment is that students take the lead in integrating assessment with learning. The teacher acts as a coach, while students repeatedly plan, revise, and reflect on their work. In so doing, they learn to provide evidence of their own learning, analyze that evidence, and give themselves and each other constructive criticism.

The limitations of portfolio assessment can be seen in the steps for preparing and scoring them. They include these drawbacks:

1. Preparing the task and scoring protocols is time-consuming.
2. Carrying out the assessment is often *very* time-consuming when compared with other forms of assessment.
3. Reliability is the Achilles' heel of portfolio assessment. We recommend using more than a single rater, plus other forms of assessment to supplement results of a portfolio assessment.

OBSERVATION

Last, but surely not least important in a discussion of performance assessment is a consideration of teachers' observations of their students. Observing and interpreting students' behavior is probably the commonest form of classroom assessment. It can be done systematically, but can also be informal and unplanned. In the early grades of elementary school when written tests are often of questionable reliability, teachers' observations, both systematic and informal, can be the most appropriate way to assess students' progress and behavior.

In these early grades, teachers observe their young charges for cognitive, emotional, and social development. The overwhelming importance of language growth in the primary grades induces teachers to focus on their students' achievement in reading, and in speaking, listening, and grasping the mechanics of writing. Normal growth in these grades moves children from simple perception to concepts of causality and classification; as students read aloud and speak, teachers listen for cues to cognitive development.

Our focus in this text on academic skills should not exclude the emotional development and growth in social skills that early childhood teachers look for. Is a child happy or sad, courageous or fearful in the appropriate circumstances? Is the natural ego-centeredness of a six-year-old so intense that he is miserable or angry when not the center of attention? Are the young learners showing signs of self-control? An ability to deal with conflict? Healthy aggressiveness rather than bullying and quarrelling? These qualities are not easily applicable to traditional tests; teachers in early childhood classrooms must look for them by observing and interpreting children's behavior.

With middle and high school students, teachers' observations are usually more informal. The systematic approach to observation commonly used for early learners does become obligatory in later grades for students in special education classes or with any student who is struggling with cognitive, emotional, or social problems. We referred earlier to the use of simple rating forms for performance assessment, but many other instruments and techniques are available. It's beyond our scope to discuss the use and merits of these means, which include anecdotal records, running records, specimen records, time sampling, event sampling, checklists, rating scales, audiotapes, and videotapes; these techniques are well described in Wortham's text on early childhood assessment (Wortham, 2005, pp. 97–105).

The great advantage of teacher observation is that it notes students' behavior, usually under natural conditions. The great concern with making judgments or forming conclusions based on observed behavior is reliability. Teachers can be unaware of the context for a student's outburst of anger, persistent sadness, or isolation on the playground. Teachers must often observe a child's behavior over time and consult with colleagues and parents to determine whether the behavior in question is typical or an aberration.

SUMMARY

- Authentic/performance assessment is the platinum standard of assessment. In performance assessment, students demonstrate their abilities by replicating the skills being measured; authentic assessment adds naturalistic and complex qualities to the assessment.
- Performance assessment requires careful attention to the preparation of the tasks and explicit decisions about the skills to be demonstrated; these may be a process or a product of the performance.
- Achieving reliable scoring of performance assessment is difficult. Rating scales and scoring guides must be designed to correspond as strictly as possible with the task. Conversely, teachers must be open to acceptable responses not envisioned by the scoring protocols.
- The benefits of performance assessment are many. Chief among them is the strong support they give to student learning.
- The two major limitations on the use of performance assessment are: they are time-consuming to devise and administer, and they are difficult to score with a high degree of accuracy.
- Portfolios are organized collections of students' work.
- Portfolios should be assessed several times over the period students are compiling them; these formative assessments are designed to encourage and guide the process. Portfolios can also be used (cautiously) for summative judgments and grades.
- The benefits of portfolios are manifold. Their primary advantage is the learning that students gain from reflecting on their own work.
- The limitations of portfolio assessment are the time demands on teachers as they periodically review and comment on the students' work and the problem in achieving strong evidence of reliability in scoring the collections.
- Observation is the most common form of student assessment, especially in the early grades. For young children, at least some observations should be made systematically, with a record kept of the results.

III

STANDARDIZED ASSESSMENT

In the chapters on standardized assessment, we attempt to answer four questions:

- What are standardized tests?
- How do teachers administer and use the results of standardized tests?
- How should students be prepared for standardized tests?
- What are the similarities and differences between classroom and standardized assessment?

For better and for worse, standardized tests are an important element in school assessment; in some schools they drive major decisions about curriculum and teaching. We offer examples of how two schools use the results of standardized exams, especially those tests mandated by the states.

We devote several pages to college admission tests, primarily the American College Testing Program (ACT) and the College Board's SAT. We point out that the excellent technical qualities of these tests can be counterbalanced by misuse of their results.

In chapter 8, we consider the validity issue: How are the results of standardized tests used? How should the results be used? We include a discussion of the thorny issue of using standardized test results to evaluate teachers' performance.

Chapter 9 deals with "test prep." We attempt to clarify appropriate ways of readying students for both the academic content and the mechanics of standardized tests.

Chapter 10 speaks to the similarities and contrasts between classroom and standardized testing. We suggest that they typically differ in their content, format, student preparation, scoring and the interpretation of results. We conclude by suggesting how teachers can gain insights into their students and their curriculum by comparing the results of standardized and classroom assessment.

7

What Are Standardized Tests?

TWO SCHOOLS' PRACTICES

We'll begin by looking at two schools that exemplify differing approaches to standardized testing.

At Elmont Memorial Junior-Senior High, in a Long Island school district adjacent to New York City, the state assessment program heavily influences the school's curriculum. Unlike some of its more affluent neighboring districts further to the east on Long Island, 23 percent of Elmont's students qualify for free or reduced-fee lunches.

In 2000, results at Elmont on the grade eight reading and writing assessment were dispiritingly low, with only 35 percent of the students meeting the state standard. On the 2005 test, 60 percent of its grade eight students met the state's criterion.

In mathematics, for the 2005–2006 school year, 75 percent of incoming students in grade five scored at Level 1, the lowest level, indicating "serious problems." But in the same year, 33 percent of sixth graders scored at Level 1, while only 4 percent of the seventh and eighth graders' scores were at the lowest level. Apparently, after just one year in Elmont's middle school, math scores of lowest achieving students climb, and by grade seven, 96 percent are either partially proficient or meet all standards.

In 2006, Elmont's high school students passed the New York State Regents' exams at the rate of 89 percent in Math A (the state average is 79 percent). In English, 92 percent of Elmont's students passed the Regents' exam, compared with a state average of 78 percent.

In 2007, 95 percent of Elmont's high school graduates received Regents' diplomas; three years earlier, that number was 64 percent. Seventy-one percent of Elmont's graduates enrolled in four-year colleges and 24 percent in two-year colleges (Elmont Memorial Junior-Senior High School, 2006). How do we explain such gains in test scores? The teachers and administrators at Elmont focus intensely on preparing for the state exams. That preparation includes Saturday morning classes for students whose classroom assessments show them lagging their classmates and test prep sessions before and after regular school hours. The school community is constantly made aware of the importance of achieving well through posters, assemblies, and hallway slogans. Elmont's faculty also use data from earlier test results to influence classroom instruction and prepare for state tests. Teachers review questions from earlier examinations; they then look at individual and class scores to determine which students may need extra help. New York's State Department of Education is facilitating this approach with nySTART, a new program that will distribute item analyses of student responses to the state exams.

What do we see in Elmont that speaks to the issues of standardized testing? First, the emphasis on test preparation and aligning classroom instruction with New York State's standards seems to have paid off in substantial increases in student scores. These results are a source of pride to students, parents, and faculty.

Second, the number of Regents' and Advanced Diplomas and the vigorous Advanced Placement Program suggests that the majority of Elmont students have mastered the basics for learning in their elementary and middle school years, and are generally well-prepared for advanced-level work. This in turn indicates that the intensive work in test preparation does not come at the expense of "critical thinking" or "higher-order skills," since these skills are required in coursework that leads to the Regents' Examinations and the Advanced Placement Program.

Third, Elmont's test preparation program has almost all the elements that many critics of testing find objectionable. Elmont administrators constantly emphasize the importance of the state examinations, and teachers focus intensively in class and in extra sessions on preparing for those tests. Teachers devote considerable time to examining previous years' results to determine whether their curricula match the test standards; they may modify their classroom instruction to enhance the alignment. In some schools like Princeton Charter School, these tactics would be largely a waste of time. But they seem to give Elmont the results it wants.

Princeton Charter School (PCS), in Princeton, New Jersey, is an elementary and middle school with some 300 students (Princeton Charter School, 2007). The student population in Princeton's public schools, including PCS, reflects the high level of educational attainment one anticipates in a town with a distinguished university and several major research corporations.

Only 5 percent of PCS students are eligible for the free or reduced-fee lunch program. PCS administers the New Jersey proficiency tests of English, mathematics, and science in grades three through eight. Additionally, in early fall, the school administers the Comprehensive Testing Program, published by the Educational Records Bureau (ERB). Certain grades within the school also participate in national competitions in mathematics and French.

Over the ten years of PCS's existence, its students' standardized test scores have been extraordinarily high, earning the commendation of the State Department of Education. In 2005, PCS was designated a national blue ribbon school by the U.S. Department of Education and, in 2007, it was listed as one of the nation's best charter schools by the Center for Education Reform. In mathematics and science, the school is consistently among the top five within the State of New Jersey.

The ERB reports in English and mathematics provide norms based on a national sample of suburban schools and another set of norms drawn entirely from independent schools. On the latter norms, more demanding than those based on a national sample, PCS outperforms its suburban counterparts and matches or exceeds the achievement of independent schools at every grade level.

What does the PCS faculty do to prepare students for their standardized examinations? Not a great deal. Upcoming state and ERB tests are discussed at a faculty meeting, primarily to ensure consistency in administrating the examinations. At this session, teachers are also reminded of how the test results will be used and that the results can have some bearing on the school's reputation in the community. Parents are informed of upcoming standardized tests and are urged to have their children in attendance, well rested, and fed; but parents are also reminded that their students' day-to-day performance in the classroom is much more important than any single examination.

In the elementary grades, PCS teachers ensure that their students are comfortable with the format of the standardized tests; the state and the ERB exams consist primarily of multiple-choice items, but both programs include essay sections as well. Students are not drilled on previous exam questions, and teachers generally urge them to "do your best" for themselves and their school, but do not imply that serious consequences will follow a poor performance on the part of individuals or a class.

PCS does very well on standardized exams and treats test preparation with a light touch. But the board of trustees, administration, and teachers scrutinize the results of standardized testing carefully. Unfortunately, the timing of the administration and reporting for the state examinations do not make the results of great benefit to the school. The New Jersey Department of Education had to expand its test development processes very rapidly, and the department has not always been able to provide timely diagnostic information, such as released test forms and item analyses, that would give teachers insights into their students' performance. For PCS, the principal value of the New Jersey testing program is that it provides the only common yardstick for measuring PCS's performance against other public schools in the state, especially against schools with similar demographics.

In contrast, results on the Educational Records Bureau examinations are reviewed carefully and reported to the PCS board in some detail. Over the December holidays, results of the ERB tests at PCS are analyzed by grade and by subgroups within each grade; these results are then reviewed longitudinally, that is, results for the same cohorts of students are "tracked" from year to year. Thus, class scores are compared with those of their peers in suburban and independent schools and, more important, with the progress of each child and achievement level within the class from year to year.

Scores of individual students are sent to parents and teachers, and parents who have concerns about the results are invited to schedule conferences with administrators or teachers to discuss their children's performance. At faculty meetings, teachers discuss test results and are encouraged to raise questions with their colleagues, especially concerning individual students whose standardized test outcomes vary considerably from their classroom performance.

Because the ERB tests provide item analyses for every student's performance, teachers can note instances of mismatches between the tests and their curricula. It is left to the faculty to decide whether any modest discrepancies warrant modifications in the content or scheduling of topics in their curricula. If test scores suggest a major mismatch between curricula and test content, the discrepancy is also placed on the agenda for the next board of trustees meeting.

What issues does the Princeton example raise concerning standardized testing? First, we note the impact of a community's high educational attainments and affluence on student achievement. (See chapter 1 on the influence of these factors.) All Princeton schools, public and independent, show high levels of average student achievement. However, averages can conceal evidence of lagging achievement on the part of some segments of the student population. So, PCS's practice of tracking low and high achieving students provides the school with important information beyond class averages.

Second, the principal purposes for statewide testing and the federal legislation that drives it are largely irrelevant to schools like PCS. State education officials, as well as Princeton's school boards, faculties, and the larger community, are well aware of the status of their schools. Results of state examinations do not stimulate significant changes or lead to penalties for such schools. The considerable time spent on administering New Jersey's testing program in Princeton serves little purpose other than setting a high standard for other school districts.

Third, drilling on released test items and other extensive test preparation at a school like PCS would be an inexcusable diversion from curricula that have proven highly successful. Once the validity of student responses is enhanced by familiarizing students with the format of exams and methods of responding efficiently to various item types, the usefulness of test preparation at PCS largely ends. The curricula in all subjects at PCS are devised with careful attention to state standards, so these standards can be said to drive the curricula. Conversely, the ERB exams are routinely reviewed to ensure that the tests are aligned with PCS's curricula, not vice versa.

Fourth, very positive results on the school's standardized testing program contribute to PCS's faculty morale and parental support. PCS is the only charter school in Princeton. Its establishment in 1996 was bitterly contested by those who felt it represented a criticism of the local public system, as, to some extent, it did. The controversy raged for several years in local newspapers and in informal gatherings within the small community. Understandably, the local branch of the state teachers' union opposed the school because PCS teachers were not required to become union members. When the school was able to demonstrate outstanding academic results, the founding parents and faculty felt their work was bearing good results, and criticism within the community diminished. The school has had a long waiting list for several years. For more information about PCS, see the school's website (Princeton Charter School, 2007).

QUALITIES OF STANDARDIZED TESTS

We will return to the issues raised in the Elmont and Princeton examples, but first, some general information and explanations regarding standardized tests. Publishers of standardized tests typically follow these procedures:

- Items (questions) are prepared according to specifications regarding content coverage, difficulty levels, and so on.
- Test items are prepared by specialists in the various disciplines, who work with professional test developers to draw on widely used texts and curricula.
- Items are pilot tested, reviewed, and revised.
- Norming administrations establish the standards for interpreting examination results.
- A standardized test has detailed instructions for administration.
- Technical manuals are provided; these contain statistics on the tests' development, as well as their reliability and valid use.

- Standardized achievement tests at the elementary, middle, and high school levels usually require several hours to administer. They typically contain many test questions; more items means greater reliability.
- Most commercial test publishers provide scoring services to their district or school clients.

Test developers make considerable use of multiple-choice questions, but increasingly, their tests contain short answers, essay questions, and other item types as well. The directions for the tests include strict timing limits for each section of the tests, ensuring that the testing is "standardized," that is, does not vary from school to school. Tests of academic achievement produced by reputable publishers are highly reliable; they are valid in representing what the test development specialists and teacher-consultants believe to be the most important and representative content of curricula across the norms group.

Norming a standardized examination is a lengthy and expensive process that tests a large representative sample of a defined group. A class of third graders' achievement in reading can be compared with a sample of third graders nationally, or all third graders within a state, or in a smaller specified norms group. Most standardized score reports also provide raw scores, which simply indicate how many items were answered correctly by each test-taker.

OBJECTIONS TO STANDARDIZED TESTS

Some educators see standardized test norms as undesirable. They say, "It's not important to learn what students know in relation to other students, but how much of requisite knowledge and skills they have mastered." That approach, called criterion referenced testing (CRT), simply reports the number of items or the percentage of the test content that each student answered correctly. In fact, most standardized tests routinely report the number of correct responses (raw scores), and teachers can readily see how much of the test material each student has learned.

What are reasonable expectations in a physics class as students take a standardized test? How much of the physics curriculum that the test-makers deemed important have these students learned? One reason commercial publishers pilot their tests before distributing them is to gain a reality check. Those who work with teachers in defining an appropriate body of knowledge report that teacher-consultants often prepare test items that are unrealistically demanding, that is, they ask not simply what students are being taught, but what the test writers wish students were being taught. State tests should be based on state standards, but those general standards can be translated into test questions that vary enormously in difficulty. The resulting tests can be unrealistically demanding and unrepresentative of what students, even in good schools, are actually being taught. Such an examination is inappropriate and does not fairly measure the knowledge and skills of the test-takers.

When developers of standardized tests pilot new items and test forms, they use the results of the pilots to create tests that include a broad range of difficulty, based on student responses to the piloted items. The resulting test is then a realistic appraisal of what high, low, and average achieving students can do; it permits teachers to consider the results in terms of their students' peers across the country. Virtually all tests are "normed" in the sense that they present a range of material that has proven appropriately challenging for a given grade level.

A second objection to norm-referenced scores could be stated: "Comparing students leads to unhealthy competition for grades. Students whose test scores are lower than those of their peers feel denigrated." It's true that tests can be viewed as a competition in which all participants do not achieve the same results. But the occasional well-meaning teacher who assigns high scores for poor work does his students a serious disservice by pretending that all achieve equally or that the results of academic assessment are unimportant. Most students aren't deceived by these pretenses, but those who are misled will leave school unprepared for the real world, or even for further schooling.

Those teachers and parents who view the unequal results of academic competition as emotionally scarring do not usually have the same objection to other forms of competitions, such as athletic contests or chess tournaments for which students first compete to "make the team," then compete in events with other teams. Those events have winners and losers and no one knows that better than the students who compete. Parents and teachers complain about, but seem to tolerate, the social competition that is a feature of every school—tryouts for lead parts in school plays or auditions for a solo part in the school choir, to name a few. Like many elements in parents' own lives, competition is a fact of life for students. Surely, it is less objectionable for students to compete for evidences of learning, that is, grades, than for prom queen or quarterback.

A third common objection to standardized tests can be stated, "Those tests just measure information, facts that students had to memorize; they don't assess higher-order cognitive skills." In fact, many commercially produced tests assess not only the various categories of basic knowledge (for example, factual, conceptual, procedural, and metacognitive knowledge) described in the revision of Bloom's *Taxonomy* (Anderson and Krathwohl, 2001), but understanding, application, and analysis, as well. Especially when these exams have essay portions, they can also assess students' abilities to synthesize and evaluate.

Assume for a moment that standardized tests measure only facts and information. In order to understand and work effectively and efficiently with mathematics, language, science, or history, students must memorize a great many facts: theorems, principles, parts of speech, vocabulary, and so on. As Michael Oakshott, a leading intellectual of the twentieth century said, "There is in all knowledge an element of information. These may be facts or rules. Before any concrete skill or ability can appear, information must be partnered with knowledge" (Fuller, 1989, p. 53).

LIMITATIONS OF STANDARDIZED TESTS

As our discussion points out, most standardized tests have much to recommend them, including that they are developed and scored with greater technical precision than is possible for teacher-made tests. One may wonder, "What's not to like about standardized tests?" There are, however, some serious drawbacks to standardized tests. Begin with the widespread antipathy nearly all of us feel toward being tested, whether by classroom teachers, state departments of education, or the Bureau of Motor Vehicles. Indeed, most of us don't look forward with pleasure to the probes and lab tests associated with a medical examination.

Second, there is no assurance that a specific class has been exposed to all the topics assayed in a standardized test; in classroom testing, teachers ask questions about knowledge and skills they have taught.

Also, a standardized test is a single snapshot, while classroom teachers are constantly observing, leading oral quizzes, correcting homework and projects, and giving written tests. It's not the standardized test that is at fault here, but the possibility that too much reliance will be placed on a single score, rather than evaluating a student or a class with a variety of assessments administered at various times during a school year.

Finally, a drawback to standardized tests is the time they require to grade and return. For every day's delay in students seeing the results of their tests, interest in the results diminishes. Additionally, errors the students have made in their responses go uncorrected for many weeks, thus reinforcing inaccurate responses. We will speak more to the pros and cons of standardized assessment later in this section.

ADMISSIONS TESTING

In this book on assessment, we point out that we are speaking almost exclusively of student achievement tests, that is, tests used to measure knowledge and skills in academic courses, whether the exams are standardized or are devised by teachers for their students.

These assessments are used to describe what a student, a class, or an entire school knows and can do in the subjects being tested. But brief mention should be made of standardized achievement tests that are used specifically for admissions purposes, especially to predict how well students will perform academically in their first year of college. Test developers attempt to define the information or skills students will need in order to master certain new information or skills; then they devise measures of how well test-takers have mastered that knowledge or those skills.

The best-known college admissions tests are the SAT, produced for the College Board, and the ACT, a product of the American College Testing Program. The ACT has always been viewed as a measure of achievement in various high school subjects. The SAT is, in effect, an achievement test of reading, writing, and mathematics. Because students' skills in these subjects are fundamental to further learning, college admission officials use scores from these tests as partial predictors of a student's academic success in the first year of college.

As we said earlier, the validity of a test is based not only on its content, but also on how the results will be used. Some uses of admission test scores by college officials are certainly legitimate; others can raise concerns about validity. Testing organizations no longer describe their instruments as "aptitude tests," but companies and admission officials continue to view them as (partial) predictors of college academic achievement. Such an understanding seems reasonable, given that courses in the first year of college assume certain levels of preparation, especially in reading, writing, and mathematics.

Scores on these tests are seen as reliable, if imperfect, predictors of college success for students. Students who score in the top 25 percent of the SAT or ACT range usually do well academically in their freshman year of college; however, the correlation of test scores with freshmen grades depends markedly on a student's response to the college environment and on the rigor of the college program. Even students whose test scores place them in the top percentile ranks of SAT or ACT test-takers may find themselves seriously challenged by a freshmen physics course at California Institute of Technology.

The majority of students who score in the lowest quartile of college admission tests, but are admitted to a college, usually demonstrate in their freshman year that they are indeed radically unprepared for college-level courses. For the middle 50 percent of test-takers, the scores appear to contribute little to admissions officials' understanding of students' readiness for college-level study. An exception occurs when a student's grades differ notably from their test scores. The divergent measures signal a need for more information about such a student's achievement level.

In general, it is reasonable to measure the verbal and mathematical skills students have acquired to estimate whether they will succeed in courses that require the same skills, presumably at a higher level, in college. But most colleges whose entering freshmen scores fall in this middle range accept all but the least academically qualified; thus it's not clear that the admission test scores contribute much to the colleges' admissions decisions.

The problem with relying heavily on standardized admissions tests is not the tests themselves. The SAT and ACT are models of careful preparation, with every item analyzed by content specialists and professional test developers. But attaching a two- or three-digit number to a student's name is a seductively easy way to describe the complexity of learning; that simple number, like most simple descriptions of complex factors, is misleading and easily lends itself to misuse.

It's also true that much can change as adolescents mature, especially in their motivation to learn. Students with mediocre, but not grossly inadequate achievement, as measured by the SAT or ACT and high school grades, can turn their academic lives around in college. Also, even in very selective colleges such students can find remedial courses in writing and mathematics that, given adequate motivation, can equip them to pass their freshman-year courses.

Admissions officials are joined by the testing agencies in emphasizing the importance of student high school grades, especially in the junior and senior year, for predicting academic success in college. The pattern of grades a student achieves in high school has better predictive value than a single score on an admissions test for the same reason that the cumulative measures of a classroom teacher will usually give a more accurate picture of a student's achievement than will a single test score. Because instructional and grading standards vary widely among high schools, admissions offices depend on standardized tests like the SAT or the ACT to confirm evidence from students' grades. But test scores, grades, and less dependable admissions measures like essays, interviews, or references are of differing value for various student populations and colleges.

What these factors in admission decisions have done is spawn two large-scale industries. One is the ubiquitous test preparation companies, counselors, and publications that have parlayed parental concerns (that their children may not be admitted to America's top colleges) into a billion-dollar industry. (See chapter 9 regarding test preparation.) Given that the undergraduate acceptance rate at schools like Harvard or Stanford hovers around 10 percent, parents' fears for their children's chances of admission are obviously justified.

The second "beneficiary" of the admissions game is the college admissions offices themselves. Institutions that receive many more applicants than they can enroll have expanded their staffs; these officials individually and in meetings conscientiously scrutinize candidates' files that are stuffed with essays, letters of recommendation, and records of candidates' nonacademic accomplishments, as well as transcripts of grades and standardized test scores. The intent of admissions staffs in selective colleges is to ensure "excellence" and "diversity" in their incoming classes. As the definition of *excellence* has broadened far beyond academic achievement, diversity has become increasingly important, even defining excellence in the minds of some admission officials.

The standardized tests that have become a rite of passage for high school upperclassmen serve some useful but limited purposes in determining admission to the 5 to 10 percent or so of colleges that are highly selective, that is, that have far more applicants than they can admit. For less-selective institutions, low scores on the SAT or ACT are also an indicator that, when confirmed by high school grades, signal college officials to be ready to offer remedial assistance to students they admit with such modest qualifications.

We should note at least one other use of admissions tests that is less defensible than those in college admissions offices. In some states, high schools are ranked by the mean SAT or ACT scores of their graduates. In virtually all high schools, these tests are voluntary, that is, the average score reflects the performance of those who choose to take the exam. A student who does not intend to apply to college, by contrast, would have no incentive to take the SAT or the ACT.

Scores of special education students who take such tests are sometimes included in the school average, but sometimes they are not. Given such exclusions, we cannot draw conclusions about a high school class from the test scores of a self-selected population of test-takers.

ADMINISTERING STANDARDIZED TESTS

Teachers usually have the dubious pleasure of administering standardized tests to their students. In addition to state assessments, the administration and monitoring of such national exams as the SAT, ACT, or Advanced Placement are also commonly done by teachers. Small wonder that some teachers complain of the tedium of reading all directions aloud prior to the tests, of keeping a constant vigilant eye on the test-takers over several hours of testing, of maintaining exact timing for the tests, and of safeguarding and returning the completed answer sheets.

Times for Testing

For many standardized test administrations, districts and schools have no choice when to administer the examinations; the dates are prescribed by the state or the testing organization and must be honored in order to prevent an exchange of information about the tests' content. When districts or schools can select the time to administer standardized tests of broad, sequential skills like reading or math, we recommend they do so about four to six weeks after the start of the school year. This period allows students to review after their summer slump, while still allowing time for the tests to be scored and results reported to schools well before the December holiday break. Such a schedule allows administrators and/or consultants an adequate opportunity to analyze the results and prepare reports for the faculty, board, parents, and the wider community. As students return after the holiday break, the reports can be distributed to the appropriate parties, and discussions can be initiated with teachers about the significance of the exam results for classes and individual students and for possible curriculum reviews. Of course, results of standardized tests administered just weeks after classes begin essentially measure student learning from the previous year or years.

The rationale for giving the tests, that is, how the results will be used, largely determines the point in the school year when they are administered. Our recommendation for testing early in the year implies that the most important use of standardized test results is to assist administrators and teachers in identifying strengths and weaknesses in the material covered by the test. Faculty can note discrepancies between the school's curriculum and the test content and can consider possible assistance to classes and students or modifications in their schools' curricula. Or, if the school has the option, administrators can look for another standardized test that more nearly matches the school's curriculum.

Many states administer their assessment programs well into the school year and report results toward the end of that year, or even during summer vacation. This schedule greatly diminishes the usefulness of the tests to schools. But legislators and state school officials are primarily interested in using the test results for summative judgments based on the average scores of schools, grades, and subgroups of students. Their principal interest is not in using test results to diagnose and remedy deficiencies in districts, schools, or individual students, but rather in pointing out each school's status in overall subject, grade, and school rankings in relation to other public schools in the state.

This timing for states' test administration and reporting is driven by the state and federal intention to use test results to encourage school improvement. This is a worthy goal for which standardized tests provide some support, but their results can be misunderstood in terms of a school's progress.

When state and federal officials use the results of tests as indicators of the status of a grade, rather than following a cohort of students from one year to the next, the evaluation of such results are problematic. If this year's fifth graders score lower or higher than did last year's fifth graders, what conclusion can officials draw? They are comparing two different cohorts of students. Regrettably, this is what the NCLB means by "adequate yearly progress." Progress should mean an increase in the *same* students' achievement from year to year. Such a judgment can only be made by comparing results from the most recent administration with those of the previous year for the same students.

However, measuring the same student from year to year also encounters some difficulties. As we mention in chapter 1, student mobility is a wild card in comparing achievement from year to year. So, even when trying to measure progress for students between fourth and fifth grade, a grade five class of twenty-five students who took a test in March 2007 may consist largely of students who were not in the school for grade four in 2006. Scores that Jon and Maria achieved in 2006 are compared with the scores of Emily and Josh in 2007. Unless school officials determine that the current cohort in grade five is at least roughly equal in achievement to that of the previous year, they may be pleased or dismayed by the status of fifth graders' learning, but they cannot make judgments about the *progress* of students in grade five. The confounding factor of high student mobility rates prevails especially in high-poverty, low-achieving classes and schools, the ones that are most likely to incur NCLB sanctions. This measurement flaw is still another reason for caution in labeling schools as "failing." It's also true, however, that a school in which, year after year, fifth graders score far below proficiency levels, is failing its fifth graders, whoever they are.

There are still other significant measurement problems in drawing inferences on teaching and learning from two test scores, but there is not a lot that teachers and local administrators can do about the limitations of state assessments beyond lobbying for improvements. Nevertheless, all educators should be aware that the point in the school year when state tests are administered strongly affects how the results can be used and the extent to which teachers and administrators, legislators, and state departments of education officials can rely on the scores' validity.

A further significant point on timing of test administrations is the duration of the exams. In general, the older the students, the longer they can concentrate on an examination. Common sense dictates that primary grade children not be tested for more than about 20 minutes without taking a break, and no more than 45 minutes to an hour in a day. This limitation applies especially to assessment that requires reading and writing, but even one-on-one interviews should be constrained by approximately the same limits. Five- and six-year-olds are aware of when they are being assessed, and of the possibility that they will be found wanting. That tension contributes to the fatigue that young children normally experience when they are required to concentrate too long on a task (North Central Regional Educational Laboratory, 1999).

The problems induced by lengthy standardized examination periods extend through middle and high school and are exemplified in the Saturday morning ordeal of the SAT. Students are instructed to arrive at SAT test centers by 7:45 a.m. and to bring snacks for the breaks that will be allowed after each hour of the four hours of testing time. From a measurement point of view, the enormous number of test items adds to the reliability of the test. But staying alert and focused for four hours, even with occasional snacks, is too much for the average teenager—or most of the rest of us. The predictable test nervousness exacerbates fatigue, which leads to errors, and such errors detract from the validity of the scores.

Again, time requirements for standardized tests are a problem that teachers and administrators can't do much about, but they should add their voices to those of students, parents, and many specialists in mental measurement who urge more humane test periods that can yield more valid test results.

Teacher Supervision

A final element to consider in test administration is just what teachers should and should not do when they are responsible for administering a standardized test. Because the point of the examinations is to give students an opportunity to perform to the best of their ability, test administrators should do everything in their power to create favorable conditions for the exams. Obviously, lighting, desks/tables, temperature, and so forth in the exam room should be optimum. To ensure fairness, administrators should adhere strictly to the test-maker's directions for seating arrangements, reading of directions, and timing of exams. If regulations permit, test administrators should periodically remind test-takers of how much time remains; if some students find themselves far behind in timing, they should be encouraged to read ahead quickly for items they know they can answer and not take time to puzzle out a solution to a problem. That is, they should not leave a block of items at the end of a section unread and blank. These directions will be further discussed in the section that follows on test preparation.

A sensitive topic related to test administration is that of cheating. Student misdemeanors can range from glancing at another's answers to the use of sophisticated electronic devices. Student cheating during a test can best be controlled by vigilant monitoring on the part of supervising teachers. A teacher who leaves the room or sits at a desk and reads or grades papers during an examination is inviting the ethically challenged student to mislead his teachers and take advantage of his classmates by submitting an invalid representation of his knowledge and skills.

More serious than student cheating is carelessness or deception on the part of teachers. Immediately after an exam, student papers should be collected; the responses should not leave the supervising teacher's possession until they are locked in the school office or another secure location. Before the exam begins, supervising teachers should check the student information pages for properly entered identification. After the exam, it is a strong temptation for a teacher to "just glance over" the answer sheets in order to gain a sense of how well his or her students have done on the exam. From glancing at students' papers, to "clarifying" a response, to a wholesale changing of answers is a slippery slope. Periodically, we read reports that some erasures and altered responses on standardized tests originate not with students but with their teachers or administrators. Predictably, these professional lapses most often occur in high-stakes testing, when schools and teachers feel that low scores reflect unfavorably on their performance and may even present a threat to their jobs.

Some professional educators have argued that what they term "pervasive cheating" proves that high-stakes testing should be abolished. We do not know how pervasive cheating is by students or school officials. Student cheating can be largely controlled by vigilant monitoring; to accuse teachers and administrators of widespread misconduct libels the vast majority of honorable professionals in our schools. Admissions officials are aware that some required student essays submitted in college admissions applications are not entirely the students' own work. But colleges continue to use essays in the admissions process that assess an important skill for success in college. We don't advocate abolishing a sport in high schools or colleges because some individual players or coaches cheat. Instead, we assume that the vast majority of teachers and coaches are ethical professionals. But we also monitor their actions, reduce opportunities for unethical behavior, and discipline the few who violate academic or athletic norms.

INTERPRETING TEST REPORTS

Standardized test reports, whether from state assessment programs or from commercial publishers, include:

- A report for each student test-taker
- A summary report for each class or grade
- An item analysis (not in all assessment programs)

These reports tend to be densely packed with information. We will give abridged examples and explanations of several forms and suggest ways they can prove useful to teachers.

Individual Student Reports

Schools receive and forward to parents a score report for each student test-taker. These reports often stimulate parents' questions, so teachers should be thoroughly familiar with the reports and be able to explain their contents.

Let's assume a multiple-choice standardized test of verbal and mathematical achievement, with subscores for each category. Subscores on the verbal section of our hypothetical report are in Reading Comprehension, Reasoning, and Vocabulary. Mathematics is broken into Calculation and Reasoning. The first chart for a student's results might look like the one in figure 7.1.

Some score reports include a student's raw score, the number of items answered correctly in each subtest, and a grade equivalent (GE), which is a score expressed in terms of a grade and a month. For example, a reading comprehension grade equivalent of 6.4 means the level at which students in the fourth month of grade six typically read. A common misunderstanding about grade equivalents can be stated as a parent's question: "My Emily in fifth grade received a grade equivalent score in mathematics of 7.4. Shouldn't she be placed in a seventh grade math class?" A GE score of 7.4 is the score a seventh grader could be expected to achieve on the test designed for fifth graders. In Emily's case, it shows that she is doing very well in her fifth grade math class, but she has not been taught or tested at a seventh grade level.

In interpreting to parents the scores on the simple chart in figure 7.1, a teacher first explains that National Norms means that their children are compared with a large, nationwide sample of students in the same grade.

Figure 7.1. Student Results

Student: Peter Rankin

Subtest	National Norms	
	%ile Rank	*Stanine*
Reading Comprehension	47	5
Verbal Reasoning	49	5
Vocabulary	70	6
Math Reasoning	38	4
Calculation	69	6

The percentile rank for Reading Comprehension, for example, shows that Peter Rankin scores as well as 47 percent of the national norms group. But be prepared for this misunderstanding: "You mean my child only scored 47 percent in Reading?" The percentile rank is *not* the percentage of items on the test that the student answered correctly, but indicates where the student stands in relation to his peers. This student is solidly in the middle of the national norms group on Reading Comprehension.

A stanine (standard nine) is simply a way of grouping scores on a normal curve into nine categories or units. Scores from 1–3 are below average, 4–6 average, and 7–9 above average. With only nine score intervals, stanines are obviously less precise than a percentage. In fact, that's an advantage of stanines; it's better to describe Peter Rankin's score on Reading Comprehension as falling in the 5th stanine, rather than at the 47th percentile. A percentage sounds so exact, but its precision is deceptive. If Peter scores at the 47 percentile, Martha at the 43 percentile, and Jason at the 54 percentile, it appears that, in Reading Comprehension, Jason is ahead of Peter and considerably superior to Martha. But all three scores fall in the 5th stanine, that is, they are essentially equal; if the students repeated the test, it's quite possible that their percentile ranks would be reversed. Indeed, statisticians require a difference of two stanines before they are willing to describe two scores as reliably or significantly different from one another. Some test reports refer to confidence bands: These are ranges of scores within which a student's true score most often falls. Like the stanine, a confidence band expresses better than a single percentage point the level of a student's achievement.

Peter's scores show him to be an average student in relation to national norms. But what if Peter's parents point out that the grades Peter receives in his classes notably differ from these test results? His teacher should be prepared to suggest reasons for the discrepancies. What are some possible explanations?

First, the national norms are low in relation to local school norms, so Peter does much better on the standardized test than his grades predict. Parents like the idea that their children's school has high standards, although in some highly competitive schools, parents may worry that stringent grading procedures will adversely affect their child's reaching the next rung on the selective school ladder.

Second, the converse; Peter's class grades are better than his standardized test scores, suggesting that local standards are lower than national norms. Most teachers and administrators will not be happy with that explanation, but recent findings from the National Assessment of Educational Progress (NAEP, 2007) suggest a worrisome degree of grade inflation in many U.S. schools. Perhaps the school's own standards are not as demanding as those on which the standardized test is based. It is also possible that some teachers consider factors other than demonstrated knowledge of the subject in assigning grades.

Before too much is made of the discrepancy between high grades and low test scores, teachers and parents should consider that Peter may simply have had a bad test day. That can happen for any number of reasons; if it occurs repeatedly, all parties involved should not rush to the judgment that "Peter just can't take tests." If Peter does poorly on a variety of classroom assessments as well as standardized tests, he's not learning what is taught in his class; the most probable explanation for that deficit, although not the only possibility, is that he has poor study habits. If Peter is one of those rare students who falls apart and can't function when he is tested, his parents and teachers should first ask whether they are contributing to his problem by overstressing the importance of test scores. Whatever the cause, accepting that "he just can't take tests" solves nothing; Peter should be helped to overcome a handicap that will seriously inhibit him all of his academic life, and beyond.

We know the previous discussion doesn't sound very sympathetic; but everyone, students included, needs to learn to deal with stressful situations. Any process by which we are evaluated will induce some anxiety; up to a point, that anxiety is helpful for students facing an exam. A challenging problem encourages cognitive activity. A student who is indifferent to his performance will not bring to the test a sufficient degree of concentration to do his best. On the other hand, a student who is overwhelmed with anxiety also cannot perform well because his high stress level interferes with his cognitive functioning. So, teachers and parents should encourage students to prepare for and concentrate on tests, but not imply that they are life or death events. A little anxiety is facilitating; great anxiety is obstructive (Noteboom, Barnholt, and Enoka, 2001).

Finally, whatever the results, parents should be reminded that the test scores are a single snapshot; they should be viewed in relation to the results of a student's day-to-day classroom assessments. Only if a standardized score is widely discrepant from a teacher's evaluation, which is the result of multiple assessments, should these other explanations be investigated.

GRADE SUMMARIES

Schools receive from their testing agencies a summary of each grade's performance. Let's examine an abridged example of the information on such a summary. Our example is a verbal subtest of multiple-choice items in writing skills. A basic description of the test and student population may include:

Figure 7.2.   Grade Eight: Writing Skills

Percentile Ranks (%ile) and Stanines (S)			
Local Norms		National Norms	
%ile	S	%ile	S
90	8	99	9
75	6	97	9
50	5	81	7
25	4	59	5
10	2	26	4

Subject Tested: Writing Skills
Grade: Eight
Test Date: 10/07
Number of Students Tested: 40
Norms: Fall

In figure 7.2, Local Norms refers to the actual scores, expressed in percentile ranks (%ile) and stanines (S), achieved by a total of forty students in two grade eight classes. National Norms are the scores of the national comparison group. Fall norms are less demanding than spring norms. Ten percent (90 percentile) of the eighth graders in this school scored as well as only 1 percent (99 percentile) in the norm group. Twenty-five percent of local students scored as well as just 3 percent of the norm group—a huge difference in favor of the local school. Fifty percent of the local school group scored as well as 81 percent of the norms group. The lowest scoring 25 percent of the local grade did as well as 59 percent of the norms group, and the lowest scoring 10 percent of the local group achieved as well as the lowest 26 percent of the norm population.

An obvious statement we can make on the basis of this report is that these eighth graders are quite advanced in writing skills, as measured by this test. Statisticians are cautious in attributing significant differences between scores, but they agree that a score difference of two stanines constitutes a real distinction. On the test described in figure 7.2, at the 75 percentile, the 50 percentile, and the 10 percentile, local students are achieving significantly better than their peers nationwide.

ITEM ANALYSIS

Not all standardized testing programs include item analyses in their reports, but we believe that, for classroom teachers, item analyses contain some of the most valuable information derived from standardized assessments. Again, we will offer a simple, abridged example. Teachers who are not familiar with this type of score report should expect to invest time in sorting out the various columns and the implications for individual and classwide results. It is time well spent.

Our example is a mathematics subtest in problem solving for twenty-two students in grade five. The top section of the report contains the usual information: the school name and grade level tested, test date, number of students tested, and fall or spring norm.

In figure 7.3 the first column below the test title is headed Item Number and Problem. The first test item number listed is 11, which is a decimals problem. The second item number is 23, a fractions problem, and so on for all the items on the test. For most categories of items like decimals or fractions, there will be numerous items on the test. The column headed % Correct, National Norms, tells the percent of students in the national norms group who correctly answered this item. Local Norms signifies the percentage of students in this class who answered the item correctly. In the example, 62 percent of the national norms group correctly answered the decimals item, as did 58 percent of the local class.

Key refers to the letter of the correct response. (A four-option multiple-choice item will label the response options A, B, C, D.)

Student Code Numbers show how each student in the grade answered the item, that is, which option he chose. In our example, we show responses for only eleven of the twenty-two students in the class. A separate list would provide the code number assigned to each student.

Reading *down* the code numbers, the plus signs tell us that student number 1 answered the three items correctly. Student number 2 correctly answered the first item on decimals, but missed the next two; for the Fractions item she chose option A, for the Number Relations item, option D.

Reading *across* the student columns, we note that item 30 on Number Relations was answered correctly by only 33 percent of the national norms group and 38 percent of the local group. Five students in our abridged example correctly chose option A, while four chose option D.

What can teachers do with this information? First, they can note the categories of math knowledge/skill (decimals, fractions, etc.) on which their individual students and the class as a whole do well or poorly in relation to national norms. Some standardized test programs release the form of a test after

Figure 7.3. Analysis of Test Results

Test: Mathematics	% Correct			Student Code Numbers
Item Number and Problem	National Norms	Local Norms	Key	1 2 3 4 5 6 7 8 9 10 . . . 22
11 Decimals	62	58	B	+ + C + A + + + C + . . . A
23 Fractions	56	52	D	+ A + + B + A + B + . . . +
30 Number Relations	33	38	A	+ D + D B + + D B + . . . D

it has been administered. If teachers have access to those actual test items, they can pinpoint precisely the elements on which their students do well or poorly. But even without knowing the exact wording of an item, the categories provided indicate pretty clearly a student's and a class's strengths and weaknesses.

Second, teachers can note the types of errors made by individual students and the class as a whole. In item 30, almost as many students chose option D as the correct response. If a teacher has the released items, she can ask why that option attracted so many of her students.

Third, if many local students score poorly on an "easy" item, that is, one which the great majority of students in the national norm answered correctly, a teacher will look for an explanation: Is the content of that item taught in his class? If yes, then some re-teaching may be indicated. If no, should that skill or knowledge be part of his curriculum? Conversely, it's a compliment to his students and teaching when his students perform well above the national norm on a category of items.

SUMMARY

- We begin with a description of how standardized test requirements can affect two quite different schools: one concentrates heavily on student preparation for the tests and on adapting school curriculum and activities to test results; the other gives attention to the tests as benchmarks for educators and trustees to confirm other evidences of the school's progress.
- The characteristics of standardized tests are described, including their preparation, content, norms, statistical information, and the test development process.
- Common objections to standardized tests are evaluated, as are the limitations of standardized test uses.
- We then discuss the importance of teachers familiarizing themselves with the content of standardized tests that their students will encounter. This information is important both for preparing students for the tests and for interpreting the results of such tests.
- We next consider the use of standardized tests for admissions decisions. We express respect for the quality of the tests themselves, but suggest the limits of their usefulness.
- We address the administration of standardized tests, with special concerns for the supervisory role of teachers and the time of year most state tests are administered and reported.
- Lastly, we consider the interpretation of test results with respect to individual students' status and progress and provide a sample of a test summary for a class.

8

Using the Results of Standardized Tests

PROBLEMS

Regrettably, the direct benefits schools and students receive from most state-mandated standardized tests are often modest in relation to the time and expense the tests require. Such a poor return on investment need not prevail, and we will suggest ways to realize more advantages from standardized examinations. But let's look first at why the results of standardized tests do not always justify the resources they demand.

When state testing programs show inadequate payoff, the cause of the problem is usually the assessment programs themselves: their purpose, timing, and the scoring and reporting of results.

The principal legislative intent behind state testing programs is to identify schools in need of improvement; state and federal regulations mandate various remedies that take years before becoming operative. These remedies range from permitting students to leave "unsuccessful" schools, to providing tutoring for at-risk students, to making wholesale shifts in staffing and school governance. Essentially, state assessment programs are summative in purpose; they collect information that permits state officials to mandate macro-changes in schools with large numbers of underachieving students. Certainly, that monitoring and pressure to improve are appropriate functions of the state, which is responsible for public schools within its borders. But summative assessments do not offer much immediate help to students nor do they assist teachers' efforts to improve their courses.

The time in the school year that state tests are administered and their reporting protocols can also preclude their providing much helpful direction to teachers. Examinations administered later than the end of the first semester do not yield reports to the schools in time for teachers to analyze them and relate them to their students and curricula. By spring, schools are pushing to cover their prescribed courses of study and simply don't have time to introduce and assess changes for individual students or a classroom curriculum. Also, when assessment scores in each subject are reported in a few broad categories, like Exceeds Requirements, Meets Requirements, and Needs Improvement, teachers and administrators don't have much information to guide them.

TEST SCORES AND TEACHER EFFECTIVENESS

An issue of great importance to all educators and legislators is the extent to which students' standardized test scores may be used to evaluate teacher effectiveness. We'll speak more to this issue in chapter 14 on accountability. Here, we present briefly the arguments, pro and con, for measuring teacher effectiveness by their students' test scores. Let's begin by stating flatly that a teacher's effectiveness cannot be appropriately measured by simply subtracting one set of average test scores from another.

If we agree that student learning is the principal goal of teaching, and that teachers have a significant role in furthering academic learning, the extent of students' gain over a period of time might properly be considered a measure of how effectively their teachers have taught them. Gain scores are calculated for a class by subtracting its average score on the previous year's test from the results on the current year's test. Or the first test may be administered at the start of a school year, and the second at the end of the year. The expectation is that a class will show the equivalent of a year's growth in the subject tested, and the norms against which local scores are compared reflect that expectation. But note the limitations of gain scores described in succeeding paragraphs.

The best argument for calculating student gain scores is that they focus on the most important outcome we expect of schooling, that is, student learning. The No Child Left Behind Act is admirable in establishing student learning as the principal criterion for success as a teacher or a school. This outcomes approach contrasts with the input model, which measures schools by the resources available to them and evaluates teachers by their education, certification, and seniority. Using student learning as a measure of teacher effectiveness seems reasonable. And it can be, if we understand that student learning as measured by test scores is just one indicator of teachers' competence and schools' effectiveness.

Why the qualification? First, a single test score does not measure all outcomes, or even all the academic outcomes that teachers try to foster. Second, calculating the academic progress of a class by subtracting an earlier test score from a later one assumes that the same students are tested on both occasions; even suburban schools experience some changes in their student bodies from year to year, or within a school year. In impoverished urban systems, it's highly improbable that this year's eighth grade includes all and only students who were seventh graders in the same school, or even the same district, the previous year. Third, the use of gain scores, especially when differences are small, places a heavy burden on the technical qualities of the tests involved, especially on their reliability.

The test items may show high validity in relation to the norming population, but fail to address important topics and areas a given class has learned. The reported reliability of these examinations will typically be high, but they will never be perfect, so some error is present in both preinstruction and postinstruction tests. If class averages on two tests are used, we learn nothing about measures of gains for subgroups that the NCLB rightly requires: students living in poverty, boys versus girls, various racial populations, and so on.

Another element of effectiveness that cannot be measured on the basis of student gain scores is a teacher's contributions to nonacademic elements of his students' lives: namely, the extent to which he assists the entire, complicated process of making a school run safely, efficiently, and effectively. These contributions include such diverse activities as tutoring students, facilitating school assemblies, mentoring student organizations, conferring with parents, and the like. True, some of these functions don't obviously affect students' academic progress, but schools can't operate without teachers who contribute beyond their classroom duties. Children must grow in various ways: physically, intellectually, socially, and emotionally. No single measure can encompass teachers' contributions to all of these qualities. As we've said repeatedly, schools should focus on furthering students' academic growth. But when a principal evaluates her teachers, she must consider the total contribution each one makes to the welfare of a school.

Randi Weingarten, the president of New York City's United Federation of Teachers, predictably and properly condemns using student test scores alone to evaluate teachers. She urges the importance of multiple measures of student learning and instructional practice. She also emphasizes the importance of teachers' competence in their subject matter, of their having a repertoire of teaching methods, and of their need for safe and orderly classrooms (Weingarten, 2007, March 18). We second this endorsement by a union head of using student test scores as *partial measures* of teacher competency.

If student test scores can contribute to assessing teacher performance, presumably they can also be used as part of a merit pay system. (For a report on merit pay proposals, see Tomsho, 2007.) Teachers' unions have not been receptive to merit pay proposals; the unions' traditional distrust of testing is augmented by their doubts about how equitably such a system would be administered.

That attitude shows some modification in an agreement between the United Federation of Teachers and the New York City schools (Gootman, 2007). That plan awards bonuses to schools based on the overall test scores of students in high-poverty schools. The unit of measurement is not individual teachers, but average scores for an entire school. Presumably, school officials hope that the rewards would persuade teachers to remain in low-achieving schools and peer pressure would persuade them to increase their efforts, with greater results in raising student achievement.

These outcomes are encouraged by having funds awarded to a school divided among the faculty by a "compensation committee" made up of two teachers, the principal, and another member appointed by the principal. A "bonus school committee" has the option to distribute the funds to individual teachers, which is surely merit pay, or to award it evenly among faculty members, but the money cannot be distributed by seniority.

We are somewhat sympathetic with the unions' continuing distaste for individual merit pay plans, with bonuses given to those teachers whose students score well on standardized tests. We are sympathetic with the unions' position because of the many variables affecting student achievement, some of which are outside the teachers' control. But we are only somewhat sympathetic, because it doesn't make sense to base teachers' salaries solely on degrees and years of experience, without adverting to whether their students are actually learning. The other contributions teachers can make to a school, for example, tutoring, mentoring other teachers, monitoring student organizations, and the like, should also be calculated in evaluating teachers and setting their salary increases.

We note that the union president's reservations about some uses of test results do not include opposition to national standards or tests. Ms. Weingarten writes, "Let's have nationwide standards for our schools. If we really want to measure how all our schools are doing, then we need a consistent, nationally recognized instrument for doing so (Weingarten, 2007, April 15).

Do all the caveats cited here mean that student standardized test results are unimportant, or cannot be used as one important indicator of teachers' effectiveness? No. If students in Mr. Maxim's science class show consistently low achievement in relation to similar classes in the school, it's sensible, even imperative, that Mr. Maxim's curriculum, assessment strategies, and teaching methodologies be monitored and evaluated. Low student achievement strikes at the core responsibility of a school and must be addressed.

Nevertheless, we repeat: Test scores alone are imperfect indicators, as is every other single measure of so complex an activity as teaching. Using student scores as the sole criterion of effective teaching is even less justifiable than using such scores as the sole measure of student achievement. For more on this topic, see chapter 14, Accountability.

IMPROVING TEST USE

In addition to moderating the problems mentioned earlier, states could increase the benefits of their testing programs if reports to schools included item analyses. (See figure 7.3.) Some states have begun sending these descriptions of the knowledge or skill each test item assesses and the option that each student chose in multiple-choice questions. This information allows faculty to compare a standardized test's content with their classroom curriculum. Teachers can then note test items on material that they did not teach and decide whether to add that information or skill to their curriculum. In formulating those decisions, teachers and administrators must be mindful that state assessment is based on state instructional standards. Teachers and schools must not ignore the legal authority those standards impose.

A more fundamental question for the majority of state tests is, "To what extent do the results provide new and useful information to state and local school officials, and to teachers?" Any state or local school administrator can readily point out the schools in which students achieve well, and those in which large numbers are failing, and teachers can do the same for their students.

It's true that the penalties attached to failing test scores have galvanized some schools to improve mediocre or grossly inadequate schools. But these successes are not widespread and will gradually decline as some states try to raise test scores by "dumbing down" the standards of academic competence. The U.S. Department of Education would probably agree that state and local officials do not learn a great deal from mandated tests that they don't already know. But the department and Congress can also assert that public school officials in some states where student achievement has long been grossly inadequate have not reacted effectively to failure; it is that failure to act that led to the No Child Left Behind Act.

Occasionally, however, test results provide information that challenges assumptions we make about the effectiveness of school curricula. In recent years, many school districts have increased the number and hours of courses, and the rigor of requirements for high school students, with a focus on core courses. In a 2007 report, the National Assessment of Educational Progress showed that high school students are taking more college prep courses than ever before and are receiving higher grades in those courses (NAEP, 2007). That's the good news. Less satisfactory, NAEP's test report on twelfth graders indicates that graduates have mediocre math scores and their reading abilities have fallen to their lowest level since the early 1990s (Tomsho, 2007). As Tomsho also reports, "States may require students to take more upper-level courses, but content is still largely left up to local school boards and varies widely." He suggests end-of-course tests to measure what is actually being taught in courses labeled "college prep."

We believe that state assessment programs could become much more effective if, while continuing their summative evaluation purposes, more states would follow the lead of a few like Arkansas, Massachusetts, and South Carolina; in recent years, these states have incorporated diagnostic and formative assessment in their state assessments, that is, they are providing better information for diagnosing and remedying academic deficiencies. When state programs do not include such helpful information, they appear to require more resources than are justified by the benefits they confer.

To be maximally effective, formative assessment reports should be prompt, preferably within a week of the test administration. (See the example from the Charlotte-Mecklenberg Schools in the preface.) Nothing even close to that turnaround time prevails in large-scale state assessment programs. Teachers do not usually receive results from such programs in time to identify learner problems and make adjustments in curriculum. But even results that arrive long after the test date, toward the end of the school year, can have some formative benefits if they yield useful information for reviewing and possibly changing the content and sequence of a curriculum for the next school year.

Commercially produced standardized tests chosen by schools and school districts usually have less waiting time for results, and schools can choose to administer them early in the school year, allowing more opportunity for formative usage. These programs usually provide a range of information and services that make their results potentially valuable to schools. While we are speaking of problems in *using* standardized test results, we should note that a major problem is *not using* them. In some schools, reports of test scores are glanced at, the bottom lines noted, and they join stacks of other reports in filing cabinets, seldom if ever to be seen again.

This neglect of insights that test results can offer often emanates from time pressures. A careful reading and analysis of voluminous reports from testing companies call for time that some principals and teachers feel they don't have. But when test results carry with them possible penalties, they tend to receive more attention. Regrettably, results from the tests that are summative in purpose are usually scrutinized, while those that could contribute more useful information to students and teachers may be neglected. Later, we will suggest methods of gaining useful analyses of standardized score reports. But these benefits will always require time and effort on the part of teachers and administrators.

Describing the worthwhile uses of standardized test scores begins with the purpose of the assessment. State officials are primarily concerned with making summative judgments about the effectiveness of their schools in meeting state standards, as measured by the examinations. To a considerable extent, school boards, local media, and the community also tend to focus on a bottom line—how well their schools are doing academically in relation to other schools in the state, especially those with demographics that are similar to their own. In this section, we refer mainly to other uses of standardized test scores, especially to assessment that provides information helpful to teachers and administrators in improving instruction and student learning. So, let's look at how various consumers of standardized test reports can profit from those reports.

School Boards

Boards of education have policymaking and oversight roles that call for an understanding of their schools' curriculum and how well students are mastering it. The chief administrator should present to the board the following information derived from standardized test reports:

- Mean scores for each grade by subject tested
- Averages by school for each subgroup specified by NCLB: race, sex, economic status, special education, English proficiency, and more
- Averages for the top-scoring and lowest-scoring one-quarter of students in each grade and school
- Comparisons of year-to-year results for subgroups, including top- and lowest-scoring quartiles

The last item, comparisons of year-to-year results for subgroups, may be the single most informative metric for trustees to consider. State departments of education are becoming sensitive to appropriate ways to measure "annual yearly progress" by requiring schools to present evidence of student growth. One state, for example, tells administrators, "Whenever possible, longitudinal data should be presented on the same groups of students (a cohort) over a period of two or more years. Comparison of this year's seventh graders with last year's seventh graders may provide baseline data, but it does not provide information on either group's growth in achievement" (New Jersey Department of Education, 2007).

These data should be available to each board member well in advance of the meeting where they will be discussed. The superintendent/principal should summarize the results at the board meeting, but members should have an opportunity to review all of the information we have listed. Note that board members who have serious concerns about a grade's or school's curriculum and test scores should inform the superintendent of their concerns before raising the issue at a board meeting. This approach is not simply a matter of courtesy to the chief administrator; as laymen, board members may misinterpret a test score, or the administrator may need time to research the issue. In either case, an advance word to an administrator can save all parties time and embarrassment at a board session.

Because the board of education is the voice of the community, its members must be able to represent the schools accurately to parents and taxpayers. The basic question that the community and media should raise about the schools is, "How well are our students doing academically?" To answer that question intelligently, board members need the information on student scores and their interpretation that their chief administrator should supply. Of course, board members should never see individual student's test results.

Administrators

All academic administrators—department heads, principals, and superintendents—should be thoroughly familiar with the test data that will be reported to the board. Administrators who actually deliver an analysis of the test results need an understanding of mental measurement that allows them to interpret the significance of the scores and implications for possible changes in curriculum, resource allocations, and the like.

The chief administrator in particular should expect questions from board members and/or the media about comparisons of the local schools with those in other districts. To some extent, such comparisons are a function of the tests' norms: Local scores will be reported by the testing agency as a percentage of scores of students in the state, the nation, or whatever group is used to constitute the norm. Often, however, board members and administrators who have a strong interest in academic achievement will want detailed comparisons of local test scores with those in schools and districts whose demographics resemble their own. Such comparisons are routine with state assessments; with commercial tests, they are only possible for districts that use the same company's assessment program.

One basic task of administrators is to provide a perspective on standardized tests to faculty and parents. This obligation begins with a reminder to teachers of the merits and limitations of the tests. On the one hand, tests based on expert opinions of what students should know deserve respectful attention, but the opinions of experts from outside a school system will not perfectly mirror a given school's curriculum.

If, for example, the middle school science program calls for studying a unit on astronomy in grade eight and a standardized test includes questions on astronomy in the seventh grade exam, neither the students nor the teachers in grade seven can fairly be held responsible for low scores on that section of the science test. Whether the district's curriculum should include astronomy in the earlier grade is an issue that faculty and administrators will want to consider. But standardized tests do not reflect all elements of a local curriculum; this is an inherent limitation and a reason for caution when interpreting their scores.

Administrators can do little about judgments made by state authorities on the basis of state-mandated tests; they can and should say to their teachers that they will not be held accountable, at least at the local level, for students' inability to answer questions about subject content that is not included in their prescribed curriculum.

Because districts are usually free to choose commercial standardized tests that most closely reflect their local curriculum, and can decide when to administer the exams and how they will analyze and report the results, administrators can learn a great deal from them about the success of their curricula. With that information, administrators and teachers can consider whether what is taught in their schools and how it is taught should be revised.

Teachers

Far more than board members or administrators, teachers can use the results of standardized tests to improve student learning. To do so, they need time to reflect on test results, and they may profit from expert advice on test interpretation. The need for time and advice suggests that one or more inservice workshops, preferably led by someone with a background in mental measurement and in teaching, would be a practical way to help teachers attend to their students' test results and learn from them. (See the suggestions in appendix B for a workshop on student assessment.)

We repeat: Teachers' own assessments and daily observations are the best source of information about their students' achievement. Teachers can use standardized tests to check their own evaluations of an individual student or an entire class. Occasionally a teacher is surprised by a high or a low test score. There are many possible reasons for a strong student doing poorly on a single exam; we can all have a bad day. Conversely, a student whose standardized test scores notably exceed a teacher's estimate of his ability can't be dismissed by saying, "she just had a good day." Students can sometimes do better than they usually do on tests, but they can't do better than they are capable of doing, assuming they did not cheat on the exam. So, students can underachieve, but not overachieve.

When a student's standardized test scores substantially exceed his classroom assessments and grades, a teacher should ask, "What am I missing here?" Apparently, this student has learned more than the teacher's own evaluation has revealed. So, the teacher should be pleased that his instruction has been more successful than he believed; of course, it would be sensible as well to ask why this discrepancy occurred.

Because a commercial standardized test reflects what a group of expert teachers believe is important in a subject, variations between the standardized test content and a local curriculum deserve careful consideration. When teachers observe such discrepancies, they should be prompted to examine their classroom curriculum and lesson plans.

SUMMARY

- The purpose of most state-mandated testing programs is summative assessment, that is, they are used to evaluate and make decisions about students, grades, and schools.
- We repeat our earlier cautions on using student test results to judge teachers' competence. The desirable element in such test use is that student learning becomes the primary criterion of a school's success. But students' achievement is also influenced by factors outside the teachers' control.
- The uses of tests mandated by the No Child Left Behind Act have had some beneficial effects, but they have been modest. The limitations of these tests' value largely result from the timing of their administration and reporting.
- Some states are trying to incorporate elements of formative and diagnostic evaluation into their testing programs. States that have introduced item analysis into their reports are notably improving the usefulness of their assessments.
- The chapter concludes by discussing the uses of test results by various school officials: school trustees, administrators, and teachers.

9

Preparing Students for Standardized Tests

PRELIMINARIES

Let's start by trying to forget, at least momentarily, all the reasons teachers and students don't like tests, especially standardized tests. Instead, let's consider why learning requires assessment. One important reason for tests is to motivate us to learn and help us improve in some element of our lives. At the level of teachers' classroom tests, that intent is obvious; with an important exam coming up, teachers will review the major elements in the curriculum and indicate to students what they should study in order to do well on the upcoming exam.

When students actually take the exam, they will again be reminded of important elements of the course; whenever possible, good teachers follow up an important assessment with an in-class review of the results. This is called teaching; it's what schools are supposed to do. Yes, teachers can and do review and point out important elements to be studied without necessarily giving an exam. But how does a teacher know whether students have, in fact, studied and grasped the essentials of their courses? How do the students or their parents determine how well the students have learned?

Learning to love tests may be asking too much, especially of the test-takers, but teachers should understand why learning cannot go forward without some forms of assessment, and they should try to communicate that reasoning to their students. At the very least, teachers should confine their complaints about tests to the faculty room; to express negative opinions to one's class is to encourage indifference to or rationalization of their test performance on the part of students.

Objection: One may concede the merits of classroom assessment as an aid to learning, but standardized tests are not based on a curriculum that a specific teacher follows. A standardized test is based on what some experienced and able classroom teachers consider to be important elements in a course. In most courses, the correspondence between local and state or national curricula will be high. A middle school course in pre-algebra, for example, will usually include the same goals, categories, and topics whether it is based on a local, state, or national curriculum. This correspondence derives in part from the national standard-setting bodies for mathematics, as well as from commonalties of content in most textbooks for pre-algebra that are in use across the country.

It is possible that a specific district or teacher may decide, for example, to teach elements of probability and statistics later in the school year than the standard pre-algebra textbooks prescribe and, depending on when the standardized test is administered, students may not yet have been taught those elements. When discrepancies occur between a local course of study and the standards on which state or commercial standardized tests are based, schools have a choice: follow the curriculum on which the tests are based, or accept the fact that their local curriculum disadvantages their students on a standardized exam. This is a no-brainer for schools that are under a state/federal threat of being labeled "failing." They must do all they can to prepare their students for state tests by adhering as closely as possible to the state standards.

These comments point to the need for local administrators and teachers to become as familiar as possible with the content of standardized tests and the curricular goals and objectives on which they are based. Teachers and students are greatly handicapped in preparing for standardized tests when the teachers have not had an opportunity to examine test specifications, item analyses, and released forms of the tests.

WHO NEEDS TEST PREPARATION?

Before beginning to prepare students for standardized tests, administrators and teachers should carefully consider the nature and degree of preparation their students, or groups of their students, need. It is certainly possible to underprepare, but increasingly, schools and test preparation consultants are overpreparing some students, especially in respect to the specialized techniques of test-taking.

Student test-takers will have varying degrees of familiarity with the mechanics of standardized tests, as well as their content. By *mechanics* or *test skills*, we mean an understanding of the characteristics of various test items—multiple-choice, essay, and so on—as well as directions for responding, time

Figure 9.1.   Test Skills and Content, by Level of Review Needed

Test-Takers	Test Skills	Content
Naive	High	High
Low Achievers	High	High
Average Achievers	Moderate	High
High Achievers	Low	Low

limits, the most effective strategies for answering various items, and other directions and test-taking techniques all students should know if their scores are to reflect their subject knowledge and skills. Content refers to what the test is measuring: reading, mathematics, English literature, chemistry, and so on. We present the grid in figure 9.1 as a guide for educators as they plan their test preparation programs

Under Naive test-takers, we include all primary grade children, any students with learning disabilities, and those for whom English is a second language. Low Achievers, even in middle or high school, need repetitions of test-taking skills. If nothing else, they will feel a little less intimidated by the standardized format. Average students are probably fairly familiar with the mechanics of the tests themselves, but could profit from reviewing and practicing helpful strategies, like when to guess, keeping track of time, and so on. High Achievers have demonstrated that they require, at most, a brief review of the mechanics and test-taking skills.

The definition of high, moderate, and low concentration must be a local decision; some schools work on preparation for a specific test an hour a day over several months, with supplementary classes after school and on Saturdays. That's certainly a high focus, probably higher than most schools can or should undertake. A low focus on preparing for a standardized test might be a single period on test skills and content.

We do not mean to equate the importance of test skills and test content. The former is a means to an end—achieving a valid score. We urge teachers to direct their greatest attention to teaching the content of the tests, but *only* if the instruction is truly teaching and learning. Teachers rightly reject test preparation that consists largely of drilling on "canned" multiple-choice questions in isolation from an instructional context. Such information factoids contribute virtually nothing to student learning, so they don't help students prepare for a test.

Preparation in the content of a test should enable students to integrate the responses into meaningful learning that they will remember and use. Consider, for example, this simple two-option item on language use:

"I wonder if (1) they're, or
(2) their coming home tonight."

This sentence allows a teacher to urge students to analyze the two words in the contraction, the differing uses of nouns, verbs, and adjectives, and so on. In studying a unit on the Civil War, students can be asked to devise their own restricted or extended essay questions and to practice outlining, writing a topic sentence, developing a thought within a paragraph, and summarizing. Practicing for the test includes test skills (timing, outlining, and so on), but the skills are incidental to the content of the history class.

The exception we make to the importance of a heavy concentration on test content is for high-achieving students. The most academically advanced students have already learned the material that makes up the greater part of a standardized test. These students will be better served by maintaining their regular curriculum, which is pitched to their high level of knowledge and skills.

"But all they're learning is how to take a test," is a common objection to test preparation programs. If preparation focuses on test content in a way that constitutes true instruction, such a program is of obvious value. When we apply for a driver's license, we study and memorize the rules of the road, and we practice under the supervision of an experienced driver. Certainly, we want to be able to pass the test, but what we are really seeking is the knowledge and skills necessary to drive safely. If we fail the test, we go back to studying and practicing until we can apply what we've learned by demonstrating an ability to drive safely.

But why should any student spend time on the mechanics of standardized test, or on learning skills that are peculiarly associated with these tests? The simplest answer is, if students follow directions and use basic testing strategies, their scores can reflect their grasp of the subject tested. Certainly, the content of an examination, the subject knowledge and skills that it tests, is vastly more important than how to take the test. The content learning is the end or purpose, understanding how to take the test is the means necessary to demonstrate that learning. If students don't read or understand directions on how to respond to a given set of items, or how to answer within the time limits of a test section, their scores will be adversely affected and will not reflect the students' mastery of the test content. It's also true that certain qualities of standardized testing that students should learn—for example, careful reading and exact attention to directions—are skills that will prove useful for a wide variety of tasks in and out of school.

TEACHERS' PREPARATION

Appropriate and effective preparation of students for standardized examinations begins with their teachers. Teachers who help students prepare for a standardized test should learn all they can about an upcoming test. State testing programs are gradually expanding the materials they share with teachers in advance of the examinations and accompanying the test reports. If detailed topic outlines of courses to be tested are available, teachers should scan them carefully. If item analyses for the previous year's exams are available, teachers can learn the topics and the number of test items related to the topic, as well as last year's test-takers' success with the items. If the state department of education provides released forms (prior years' exams) or at least sample items from earlier versions, teachers should obtain and review them.

We will briefly describe a full-scale test preparation program, suitable for naive and low-achieving students, mostly suitable for average-achieving students, and far more elaborate than high-achieving students need. Depending on the amount of time allocated for test preparation, the steps recommended here should be spread out over time and should be repeated several times for students most in need of preparation. Note that strategies for responding to various types of test items are discussed in this book's part II, Classroom Assessment.

Steps in Student Preparation

1. Explain and describe the test: its purpose, length, general content, when the results will be reported, and how they will be used. Show students a copy of a released form of the test, if one is available. Tell students what to bring to the test and, if applicable, when and where to report.
2. Read, explain, and give examples of the directions for responding to various types of questions.
3. Read aloud some sample questions, using relatively easy items, and ask the group as a whole to respond. Ask students to explain the rationale for a correct answer and why other responses are wrong. Gradually increase the difficulty level of the items and observe topics or test skills with which some or most students are having trouble.
4. Administer a section of a test under standardized testing conditions: directions, time limits, manner of responding, and so on. If released forms of the upcoming test are available, use a section from those forms. Commercially published books exist for many major examinations like the ACT, SAT, or Advanced Placement; use a section from these if it is appropriate for a class's purposes.

   In reviewing results of this "mini-administration," concentrate first on students' grasp of the test skills required in the section. Discuss the strategies that students used in responding to the items. For example, did they read all options for a multiple-choice question before choosing a response? Did they keep moving through the section, noting items they could not answer immediately and reaching the last item in the section, then returning to difficult questions in the time remaining? Did they guess intelligently, first eliminating any options they believed to be incorrect?

5. Move on to the content of the test as soon as students seem even moderately well versed in test skills, understanding that, for the lower-achieving students, the test directions and strategies should be repeated several times.

   All classroom teaching should be "content," but for the narrow purpose of test preparation, teachers must focus on the content that is most likely to be tested. The major national test programs provide an abundance of information on the topics they cover. Note that copyright laws prevent most publishers of test prep books from using "authentic" items that were administered in earlier versions of the examination. If the company that produces the test also publishes test preparation materials, teachers should use these authentic forms and items. The College Board, for example, sells books with several released forms of its SAT and AP examinations.

   For state testing programs, teachers should review all materials the state department releases, including outlines of the content, item analyses, sample questions, and, in some states, released forms of earlier versions of the test.

6. If an examination's prep materials have examples of essay questions with various levels of student responses and explanations of the readers' scores, teachers have a convenient resource for preparing students for a writing portion of an exam. (This is true, for example, for the Advanced Placement examinations.) For test preparation purposes, teachers should distill the principal effective strategies for responding to a requirement for a relatively brief essay in a very limited span of time. This is not an English teacher's ideal for teaching writing, but the ability to create several reasonably coherent and intelligible paragraphs on a topic is a skill that students will certainly need in further studies and will need to use in many careers.

7. In preparing for exams that include reading passages, followed by multiple-choice questions, teaches should again focus on any materials available that provide items drawn from earlier versions of the test. First, read aloud the questions based on a passage. Then, allow students time to read the passage silently, placing a pencil check mark where they see what appear to be references to the questions.

8. In reviewing responses to mathematics items, it's easy to see when students make simple errors of calculation or whether they simply don't know how to perform basic arithmetic skills or don't understand fractions and decimals, algebra, or geometry. A lack of these basic skills

and knowledge demands intensive review and practice in the math topics that will appear on the exam.

9. In helping students prepare mentally for any important exam, teachers should try to strike a balance between exaggerating the effects of the exam results and minimizing them. In a school whose academic reputation is suffering, or that is under threat of sanctions for low achievement, scores on state examinations can have an impact on teachers as well as students and parents, so all parties should encourage students to give the examinations their best effort. Last-minute cramming is seldom useful, especially for standardized tests, so students should be encouraged to get a full night's rest and a good breakfast before the big exam.

These steps sound like a pretty full program; as such they may be taken as an endorsement of spending a lot of time and effort on test preparation, at least for some teachers and students in some schools. Note that the amount of preparation should be determined by the varying needs of students. But yes, for many students and entire classes, these recommendations constitute a considerable block of time. What are the costs of our suggested approach, that is, what do teachers give up in order to carry out an intensive test preparation program? A common response is, "Instructional time; we can't teach our subject curriculum if we must spend a lot of time in test preparation." Let's consider that objection.

The curricula for school courses do not usually include strategies for taking tests. So instruction in test-taking strategies is indeed time away from the usual curriculum. We emphasize that "test-wiseness" should be by far the lesser part of preparing for a standardized test, with the greater effort devoted to the test content. The content of a standardized test covers essentially what a typical subject curriculum will include. That commonalty is especially true for state-mandated tests, which are based on state standards; local curricula should reflect those standards.

We urge teachers to become as familiar as possible with the principal topics examined on upcoming state tests so they can consider whether, or when and how, to integrate the topics into their classroom instruction. Preparation for the demands on students' knowledge and skills in a test is then appropriate classroom instruction. "But that's just 'teaching to the test,'" some will complain. Admittedly, the sequence of a teacher's lesson plans may have to be revised, and some may complain that their professionalism or creativity is inhibited.

But finally, the obligation in every profession is to do what is best for clients; for a physician, a lawyer, or a teacher, that usually means following the rules and norms of accepted practices in relation to their clients' needs. A skilled professional respects those norms, while also being aware of cases in which the usual practices should be varied. State tests are based on state-approved standards of instruction, so teaching to the test means teaching to state standards. That's appropriate, even obligatory, for all public school teachers.

The curriculum on which a well-developed standardized assessment is based represents a consensus of a group of veteran teachers. An experienced teacher may properly supplement the standards on which a test is based. But most students will be appropriately instructed when their teachers base their classroom instruction largely on the standards used to design a standardized test, especially a state-mandated one.

SUMMARY

- Teachers and students should be prepared for assessments for several reasons:

    Appropriate test preparation is good instruction.
    The results of both classroom and standardized tests can influence student grades and promotion, so the tests deserve the students' best efforts.
    In preparing students, as well as by analyzing test results, teachers can learn when the class can move further in a course, or when some elements need to be re-taught.

- Test preparation should be based on the degree of preparation certain groups of students need. The preparation in course content should be based on important elements in the curriculum, not on isolated test items.
- "Who needs test prep" is the next section. We distinguish the needs of naive test-takers and low, average, and high achievers.
- Preparation for the tests' content, the major learning intended in the course, differs radically in importance from preparation for the test process, the mechanics and techniques of taking tests.
- We present a nine-step program for preparing students for standardized tests. The program is a full one, suitable for some students and schools, but too extensive for others.

10

Classroom Assessments and Standardized Tests

COMPARISONS AND CONTRASTS

Standardized tests have some of the same characteristics as the assessments that classroom teachers prepare. The following paragraphs describe how these modes of assessment resemble and differ from each other.

1. The content of a classroom assessment is typically restricted to knowledge and skills that have been taught within the previous few days or weeks. Of course, major tests before a grading period or at the end of a semester will cover more material. But through interim assessments, teachers test the most important elements of what they have recently taught. Standardized tests usually cover knowledge gained over a year; in some subjects like language arts, a test measures the grammar, vocabulary, and analytical skills that students have learned cumulatively over several years. The curriculum on which a standardized test is based is a body of knowledge and skills that a group of experienced teachers in the subject judge to be important. As mentioned, the classroom teacher's curriculum usually will not, and probably should not, deviate greatly from that devised by colleagues for standardized tests.

2. Preparation for an important classroom test is pretty straightforward: Teachers indicate and review major topics that will appear in the exam and remind students where they are covered, whether in a text, class notes, or supplementary materials. Students should receive information on the approximate length of the test and what kind of items will appear on it.

A standardized test calls for a different sort of preparation. In addition to determining as much as possible the content of the test and ensuring that students have been instructed in that content, teachers should also spend at least a little time making sure that students understand the format, item types, time restrictions, and so on that a standardized test requires.

3. Classroom assessment can take many forms. Some of teachers' most valuable insights into their students' achievement will come through informal observations over a period of time. A brief quiz on a previous day's learning need not follow specific protocols.

   An examination that counts heavily toward students' grades should be administered under some of the same strict conditions as those required for a standardized test. That is, students should be given directions on how to respond and how much time they will have. Before the test begins, an opportunity should be provided for student questions; after testing begins, no further questions or directions should be allowed. During the administration, the teacher actively monitors the room; at the end of the test period, she collects the papers immediately and keeps them securely in her possession.

4. Scoring a classroom test will vary with each type of assessment. For a formal, written test, teachers look for mastery: how much of the tested material each student knows. Scores may be expressed as the number of items correct or wrong in a math or spelling test, the number of errors as well as commendable elements in an essay, or partial credit may be given for some responses in a science or history test. Those marks may be translated into a percentage, a letter grade, or simply into pass or fail.

   Standardized tests are primarily scored on the basis of norms, that is, local students' responses are compared with a defined peer group, for example, a national sample of grade eight math students, or all eighth grade math students in a given state. Standardized test scores are distributed along a normal curve, so any student's score indicates mastery of the material only in relation to other students' achievement. Scoring and grading on a normal curve is not practical for a classroom teacher; the relatively small number of items and of test-takers in a class does not justify such a distribution of scores. The number and difficulty of items that each student masters is the best indicator of each one's achievement; such scores also enable teachers to judge whether their tests are overly difficult or too easy for their classes.

5. In interpreting and evaluating the results of classroom assessment, teachers have the great advantage of placing results in a context of various assessments over a period of time. If a student does poorly on a weekly math quiz, a teacher will know whether that score represents the student's typical performance, whether the student was absent several days during the week, and so on.

If an entire class scores low on a classroom exam, a teacher will usually know whether the problem is a lack of preparation on the students' part, or insufficient instruction by the teacher. Neither of these rationales is of much help in interpreting standardized test results. Scores are primarily defined in relation to the test's norms groups, although most standardized tests also provide raw scores: the number of items correct in each section of the exam. Without a detailed content outline or item analysis, a teacher can only make an approximate judgment of how much of the test material her students have mastered.

6. The usefulness of results is a critical element in judging the merits of any assessment. Classroom assessments make up the most valuable set of tools in evaluating student performance; their value depends heavily on teachers' careful accumulation of results from various forms of assessment administered over a period of time. An evaluation of a student's or a class's achievement should derive primarily from a teacher's review of and reflection on many indicators of learning. Then why are standardized test results useful? Because a teacher's understanding of his students' mastery of what he has taught can benefit from a larger, more objective context. A standardized test tells the teacher what many of his peers teach, and how well his own students have learned that content in relation to other students at their grade level. The standardized test offers an objective complement to the individual teacher's evaluation of his students and his teaching.

INTEGRATING RESULTS

How can teachers combine the insights from both classroom assessment and standardized test results to improve student evaluation and instruction? Standardized tests can provide an external, objective report of individual and class achievement to compare with a teacher's own evaluation, which is based on many assessments. Experienced teachers will usually not find dramatic discrepancies between a class's results on a standardized exam and their own evaluations of the class. However, subscores on a standardized instrument can sometimes reveal strengths or weaknesses in various topics.

Before simply writing off differences to measurement error or variations between the standardized test content and their own curriculum and assessments, teachers will want to ask the following:

- In general, do my students' scores on the standardized test agree with the results they achieve on my classroom assessments?
- Are my students' standardized scores generally satisfactory in relation to the test norms, that is, the achievement of their peers, given the demographics and previous preparation of my students?

- Should I give more attention in class to topics on which my students generally score lower than the standardized measure?
- Are my assessment results for students of high, low, and average achievement significantly higher or lower than those of the norm groups used by the test publisher?
- On the standardized test, do subgroups in my class—minorities, classified, ESL students—show notable differences from my evaluation of their classroom performance?

SUMMARY

- Teacher-prepared assessments differ in several respects from standardized tests:

  The content of teachers' own assessments is based on the curricula they have taught. Standardized tests are based on content that committees of teaches and test developers consider appropriate.
  Preparation for standardized tests differs in a number of ways from that for classroom tests.
  The format, administration, content, and scoring of standardized tests are rigorously prescribed. In contrast, teachers can create and use many modes of assessment in their classrooms.

- Both standardized tests and classroom assessments can provide useful information to students and their parents, as well as to teachers, school officials, and the wider community.
- Classroom assessment is a frequent, ongoing activity, permitting teachers to evaluate the results of any single assessment in a larger context of student achievement. A standardized test is a single snapshot of achievement.
- In their own assessments, teachers look for the extent their students have mastered a subject. Standardized test scores compare an individual's or a class's scores with a specified peer group.
- By carefully studying standardized test results, teachers can gain an understanding of their students' achievement that complements information gained from classroom assessments.

IV

GRADING AND REPORTING

This section describes the process of translating student assessment results into grades, and recommends ways of reporting the grades to students, parents, and other appropriate parties.

We begin by describing the variety of symbols schools use to describe student achievement, from very specific percentiles to a general grade of pass or fail.

Faculty should agree on the weight to be given scores on final examinations; those single measures should not overbalance the results of multiple assessments during the grading period. Teachers and administrators should also be in general agreement on the number or percentage of As and Fs they can assign.

A valid and fair grade for achievement in a course should reflect only a student's mastery of the knowledge and skill taught in the course. Grades should be based on the results of multiple assessments, weighted according to their importance.

Students and parents should be informed of all elements that contribute to the grading process. Teachers should immediately report to administrators and parents any serious concerns about their students' academic performance or behavior. Routine periodic reports should consist of brief summaries that contain no surprises for students or parents.

School administrators have several responsibilities for grading and reporting: to monitor grades assigned by teachers, to support teachers through providing in-service training in assessment, to mediate controversies with parents over grades, and to report grade and schoolwide assessment results to the board and the community.

11

Summative Progress Reports

WHAT'S IN A GRADE?

A grade on a test, a paper, or a project summarizes how well a student responded to the questions or assignment. A grade on a periodic report for parents integrates the results of a student's performance over various classroom assessments.

The grade a student receives on a classroom assessment usually represents the sum of his correct answers. This rating may be expressed in various ways:

- A raw score—15 of a total of 20 items were answered correctly.
- A percentage—85 percent correct (some items may count more than others).

Or, a less specific symbol may be used:

- A letter—A through F
- Pass or fail
- Excellent, Satisfactory, Needs Improvement; or the categories used in the National Assessment of Educational Progress: Advanced Proficient, Proficient, and Basic.

Note, however, that for children in primary grades and those in special education, narrative reports can replace or supplement the more traditional metrics. For descriptions and examples, see Wortham (2005, pp. 230–34).

The traditional student report, usually issued every six to nine weeks, attempts to integrate the results of all assessments within the grading period. These evaluations become part of a student's record and are important in informing parents, and the students themselves, on how well students are achieving. In deciding on a summative grade, teachers assign varying degrees of importance to their observation of students' classroom performance, homework, weekly quizzes, and more formal tests.

Because written tests with many items tend to be more valid and reliable than other single examples of student work, they are a major source of information; the danger is that they can overpower other pieces of evidence of student achievement that, cumulatively, are equally or more reliable and valid than a single, formal test. A common example is the "final exam," in which teachers review important elements of a semester or a full year's instruction. If teachers have compiled a record of each student's academic performance over a marking period, the single score on a final exam should not count more than 15 to 20 percent of a student's semester or final grade. When a score on an examination accounts for a third, a half, or more of final grades, students' cumulative records of achievement over a grading period are overshadowed by a single measure.

The practice of largely or exclusively determining course grades by means of a final examination may be a carryover from college and graduate school practices. In some institutions of higher learning, the final exam is virtually the only measure of students' grasp of course material. But teachers in elementary, middle, and high schools have other resources on which to base their grades. Let's be clear that we believe final exams are a good practice in high schools and, probably, in middle schools. They provide a basis for reviewing the high points of the course and a motivation for students to fix those points in their minds. We simply urge that, in awarding periodic grades, a single measure not be allowed to overwhelm the results of teachers' own multiple assessments.

Some schools have set rules for reckoning a score on a final exam into a students' semester or year-end grade, and some uniformity within a school is surely desirable. But a teacher who employs a variety of assessment measures throughout her course has compiled a record that is more valid and reliable, that is, more accurate and fair, than one who bases her grade largely or exclusively on a single test, no matter how comprehensive and well prepared that test is.

Should teachers incorporate students' scores on standardized tests into their final grades? It's true that the majority of standardized tests are well-designed instruments with high reliability. But the probability that any given class of students has not been exposed to some information required in the tests makes them inappropriate contributors to a student's grade point average. That number, a vitally important measure in some highly competitive high schools, should reflect only student achievement on material assigned and taught in their classrooms. Of course, students' permanent records should include distinct scores for standardized tests they have taken and parents should be informed of those results.

HOW MANY As?

Some schools mandate the proportion of students in a class who may receive a specific grade, thus creating an asymmetrical curve. For example:

Approximately 15 percent of students may receive an A
35 percent may receive a B
30 percent C
15 percent D
5 percent F

The merit of such a system is that it acts as a check on teachers who tend to grade their students very high or very low in relation to the practices of other teachers in the school. If, in a classroom of average students, every student receives an A or B, it's possible that the course content is set too low for the students' abilities. Conversely, if half of a class is graded D or F, the course standards and the teaching and assessment practices need to be examined. Of course, other explanations are conceivable: on the one hand, a class may be made up of exceptionally talented individuals, or it may be one in which most students just don't study the material that is taught.

Setting some guidelines for awarding grades makes good sense in terms of communicating with parents, who are confused by extremes of severity or leniency in grading. As is usually the case, virtue lies in the middle, so teachers need to strike a balance: quotas for As and Bs leave no room for exceptions in terms of students' abilities and efforts (or those of their teachers). Very low grades for students who are at or above average in ability and effort are not evidence of "high standards," but raise questions about a teacher's own performance and understanding of his students.

True, some courses are intrinsically more difficult than others, and are understood to carry high standards of achievement. Students who enroll in honors programs, Advanced Placement, or International Baccalaureate courses, for example, expect the requirements to be more extensive and demanding than the standard program. Those requirements are spelled out in the course descriptions, and some high schools demand prior evidence of strong achievement and/or motivation before allowing students to enroll in these demanding classes. Again, grades in these programs should reflect student achievement, not the difficulty levels of the courses.

This issue of the validity and fairness of grades deserves a few more words. Once administrators and teachers agree that the proper basis for calculating students' grades is the extent to which they have learned the content of the course, administrators should be alert for evidence that a teacher's grading practices show wide discrepancies from those of the great majority of her colleagues.

A problem with one or a few teachers does not necessarily call for enacting a schoolwide rule. The administrator and teacher can first compare the class grades in question with those the same students receive in other classes, and with their scores on standardized examinations. If they differ widely, the teacher's curriculum, assessments, and expectations should be examined.

A teacher should have an opportunity to explain why her classes should be considered an exception to school norms. If that explanation is not persuasive, that is, if the administrator and perhaps some of the teacher's peers conclude that the information given to students and their parents is unfair and misleading, the administrator may then properly set grading guidelines for the errant teacher to follow. Even these norms are best stated in terms of ranges, rather than a cutoff point. So, for example, 10 to 20 percent of the class would receive an A, 20 to 35 percent a B, and so on.

HOW MANY Fs?

If every student in a class will usually not receive an A on an exam, should any student receive an F? The arguments against assigning failing grades are: One, it's discouraging to students who often are most in need of academic encouragement. Two, when a failing score on a test or paper is averaged into a student's report card it is difficult to achieve a satisfactory grade for a marking period, even when other grades are adequate. So, a failing grade can have the effect of reducing student motivation to improve.

The contrary arguments focus on the importance of giving students and parents accurate, objective feedback on academic performance. A teacher may say, "If, on a test of ten items, a student answers only three correctly, his score/grade should be thirty. To assign a higher score would be misleading."

Call these the subjective versus the objective approach to low grades—feelings versus facts. Our view is that the best practice falls in the middle of these positions: teachers should consider how their students feel and react, as well as the academic knowledge and skills they demonstrate. We recommend that the low point on a range of scores on a test be no more than five to ten points (on a 100-point scale), below the "pass" level. So, if Josh answers only three of ten problems correctly on a test, and the minimum pass score is 65, we suggest giving Josh a grade of 60 percent on the test. In correcting Josh's paper, his teacher will clearly note the items that Josh got right or wrong, so it will be obvious that Josh did not "earn" a 60. Obviously, this practice does not entirely avoid the negatives previously mentioned. But it seems to us a reasonable compromise between emphasizing students' feelings over facts and a hard-nosed approach that can result in lowered student motivation.

VALID AND FAIR GRADES

A grade assigned to a test, a paper, or on a report card should be a valid one. "Well sure," teachers say, "no argument there." If a grade represents the extent to which students have mastered the content of a course—how much U.S. history or chemistry or Spanish they have learned and their skill in applying that knowledge—then the grade, to be valid, must reflect *only* that knowledge and those skills. Still no problem? Consider some factors that should *not* influence a grade.

- Effort: A student who tries hard deserves praise and credit. The credit he receives for his effort, however, should not be commingled with credit for his achievement in the content of the course. Conversely, a student who is "lazy," or "just doesn't study," but who achieves a high grade on various assessments deserves full credit for the learning she has demonstrated. Such a student and her parents need to hear from her teacher that she could achieve still better, given more effort. (It's also possible that the student needs a more demanding curriculum.) A score or grade in an academic subject should be based strictly on the quality of a student's grasp of the subject matter, not on attendance, attention, or other nonacademic criteria.
- Improvement: Roberta and her parents are pleased to learn that she has "shown improvement in her class participation and her grasp of fractions and decimals." Presumably, Roberta's test grades and the quality of her classroom participation will reflect her improved knowledge and skills. But because teachers are naturally well disposed toward students who show improvement, there is a temptation to use "improvement," like "effort," to boost a student's grades. If the improvement is real, Roberta's assessments will show that growth, and she should be praised for her efforts. No additional reward in terms of scores or grades is appropriate.
- Ability: This quality cuts both ways in grading. A student who hasn't shown much grasp of course content does "better than expected" on a test. Give her a few extra points to encourage her? A student with a

strong record of achievement produces a mediocre paper. Give him a D to motivate him? No, and no. Both students should receive directions and encouragement by their teacher's comments on their papers or in a discussion. But a valid grade is a grade is a grade; it is a teacher's description of a student's knowledge and skills as shown by one or many assessments. (Note that this dictum doesn't exactly match our prior comments on avoiding extremely low grades on a test.)

- Behavior: This quality is a critically important one for every student and for the conduct of a class. The class clown or the constant talker is indulging in antisocial behavior that must be modified by the consistent, cooperative efforts of parents and teachers. But when the most irritating student in a class pulls a score of 98 percent on the quarterly exam, it is unjust and counterproductive to reduce his score because of unsatisfactory classroom behavior. What about his grade for the entire course? If the course title is Biology, and the standards for grading the course make no reference to classroom behavior, a valid grade will consider only evidence of knowledge and skills in biology.

Of course, a single test ought not be the only evidence contributing to a semester grade. Homework, papers, class recitation, special projects, and other evidence of achievement should go into setting the summative grade. But a grade in a subject should not be a reward or penalty for behavior; a grade is a teacher's best, objective judgment of a student's mastery of the subject.

However, cheating on a test or plagiarizing a paper invalidates a score or grade. For a first-time or minor offense, teachers may choose to give an Incomplete and require a make-up test or rewriting a paper. Some teachers simply assign a Zero for cheating on a test or paper. That grade may be justified in terms of the single assessment, but a zero score that is factored into a student's final grade will probably lead to an F for the course despite other satisfactory scores on classroom assessments.

Each student's grades should be assigned primarily on what he has learned of the material, not in relation to how well other students have performed. In other words, the criterion of each student's grade should be his mastery of the course content as assessed.

We waffle a bit by using the word *primarily*. The best-prepared students usually earn the top grades, so comparing students with their classmates will reflect their relative grasp of course content. What we are warning against is setting class standards and grades based on the performance of the highest or lowest achieving students in the class, rather than on the academic standards of the course itself.

SUMMARY

- Student grades on a report card are a summary of the results of teachers' assessments over a grading period.
- Teachers and administrators in a school should agree on what constitutes evidence of student achievement at each level of the grading scale and apply that standard consistently.
- Grades can be expressed in various ways: letters, numbers, or broad descriptions like Excellent, Satisfactory, and so on. Certainly for elementary grades, and probably for middle school, descriptive terms are preferable. Teachers should generally avoid the seeming precision of reporting summative evaluations with percentages.
- To be valid, a score or grade should reflect only what it purports to measure. Elements like neatness, spelling, effort, and so forth should be noted and perhaps, graded separately. But a grade in a subject should represent only a student's demonstrated knowledge and skills in that subject.

12

Reporting Results of Assessment

GUIDELINES FOR TEACHERS

Teachers report to students, parents, and administrators in varying detail and at differing intervals. Students are the most frequent recipients of feedback from teachers on their academic achievement. That feedback derives from scores on written tests, as well as other sources such as oral questioning in class, contributions to classroom discussions, homework, projects, and papers.

We've stated that student behavior should not influence course grades, and we reiterate it here. But teachers do have a responsibility for children that goes beyond their concern for academic achievement and assigning grades. They are obliged to observe, and sometimes intervene and report certain types of behavior. This responsibility is obviously, but not exclusively, the province of those who teach young children—those in the elementary grades. A teacher who observes consistent withdrawal and absence of normal emotional response in a child, or a teacher who sees a child being bullied in the corridors or on the playground is ethically obliged to consider how he can most productively help these children.

Teachers are not therapists, and should be cautious about "diagnosing" and "treating" persistent problems in their young charges. But one reason they became teachers is that they care about the physical, emotional, and social development of children, as well as their intellectual progress. They also have opportunities to assess students' behavior in ways that others, even parents, do not. Their intervention will usually be directly with a child, and for minor problems, no further action is called for. For recurring or serious misbehavior, intervention should include a *prompt* report of the problem to an administrator and to parents.

Research on successful job performance points to the enormous importance of "character," or work habits. Patience, persistence, punctuality, hard work—these correlate more highly with success on a job or in a profession than does academic achievement (Duckworth and Seligman, 2005). Of course, for students, strong academic achievement is a version of success on the job. Students with good work habits tend to be successful in academic achievement. But the importance of these character factors reminds us that the bright student who doesn't study and is "good at taking tests," may receive good grades in his early schooling; but unless he develops habits of regular study in which he perseveres, he will not be equipped for later, more demanding intellectual work or for the world of work.

The importance of working hard at one's studies reminds us how pernicious is the practice of overpraising students who, in fact, have neither tried hard nor achieved well. However well meant, ignoring the results of assessment by calling mediocre work excellent, or failing work adequate, is an enormous disservice to students. It's an understandable, if shortsighted reaction on the part of a student when she says, "Why should I study hard? I get good grades and praise from my teachers without doing much work." Clear, straightforward feedback on students' behavior, whether concerning their social interactions or their work habits, is also an appropriate element in teachers' reports.

We encourage teachers to follow these guidelines in grading and reporting on students' academic progress:

1. Inform students and parents of all elements in the grading process.
2. Use multiple assessments in calculating grade reports.
3. Base grades only on demonstrated achievement of course objectives.
4. For brief or informal assessment, provide students with feedback, but don't assign a grade (formative, rather than summative assessment).

GUIDELINES FOR PARENTS

Parents are just as concerned as their children—often more so—about the students' school progress. Teaches have a legal and ethical obligation to report to parents at regular intervals on students' academic learning, and anything else that teachers have observed and parents should know.

Especially in elementary and middle school, routine written reports are often supplemented with parent conferences, with interim notices of concerns teachers have about their students' performance, with telephone calls, and by e-mail messages to parents. These teacher-initiated communications can materially improve parental understanding of their children's school life, and engender cooperation in their children's learning.

Sometimes, parents believe that faculty members are not aware of, or are not dealing appropriately with, some aspect of their children's schooling. Teachers and administrators welcome reasonable expressions of these concerns and opportunities to discuss them; working together, parents and teachers can clarify and resolve most difficulties students are experiencing. Such problems should be called to the attention of teachers and administrators because they can do something about them. Discussing the problems with other parents tends to exacerbate, rather than resolve the issues.

But we urge administrators to set and enforce reasonable expectations for both parents and teachers in terms of how much of teachers' time should be devoted to writing to and speaking with individual parents. For a few parents, reasonable concern can escalate into attempts to micromanage their children's school experiences. Such a situation is unfairly burdensome to teachers and counterproductive for the object of all this attention, the children.

We also urge parents to be mindful that, especially in elementary and middle schools, teachers are often required to prepare periodic reports that call for anecdotal comments as well as summative grades. These remarks are expected to be insightful, personal, and positive; needless to say, they must be flawless in terms of grammar and spelling. For those who teach twenty-five students a day in self-contained classrooms, these written reports are surely a substantial effort; but narrative reports can help parents better understand their young children's early school experiences, so the effort to prepare such reports in elementary grades is probably time well spent. Yet even in the elementary grades, some teachers of art, physical education, or music may teach a hundred or more students every day. These teachers should assign a grade, but should not be expected to write narrative reports for every child.

For teachers in middle or high school who probably meet as many as five classes of twenty or more students a day, the many hours they must devote to preparing written descriptions of each student's performance do not seem justified. Speaking from the authors' viewpoints as teachers, administrators, and a parent, we believe the vast majority of these anecdotal reports to be unproductive in relation to the drain on teachers' time and energy.

If a student's parents need to be informed of a current or looming problem, parents can expect that communication to take place immediately, not at the end of a grading period. For parents who check their children's homework, see their graded tests and papers, and who receive periodic course grade reports, the only effect in daily or very frequent communications with teachers is the feeling that they, the parents, are in charge of their children's daily school program. This attitude is not only false, it communicates to a child the message that he should be the principal focus of his teachers' attention, and encourages him to supply "grievances" that fuel parental interventions.

It's also true that some teachers wish for more, or even any, communication with parents. Parents who are unresponsive to attempts to inform them and gain their cooperation frustrate the efforts of the school, to the detriment of their children. Some children bring crippling deficits to school; they do not have adequate emotional, intellectual, or social development, and are not motivated to study. Without sustained parental support, it's extremely difficult for schools to cope with persistent learning or behavioral problems of students. This is a reality that critics of "failing schools" can fail to acknowledge.

GUIDELINES FOR ADMINISTRATORS

Administrators also have professional responsibilities for reporting students' progress. Probably their most important contribution is not in submitting reports, but in ensuring that their teachers have opportunities to learn the basics of good assessment and evaluation of students' progress. Workshops on techniques and uses of classroom assessment and interpreting standardized test results can yield a substantial payoff in student learning and curriculum improvement, as well as in improved reporting to parents. (See appendix B for an example of a workshop.)

But, as educators know, in-service workshops have little impact on teaching without sustained follow-up activities. For programs in assessment, follow-up activities could include faculty meetings devoted to assessment before or after a major testing period, and a system of formative review of teachers' written tests and oral questioning by a supervisor or experienced peer.

Besides helping teachers to improve their assessment skills, administrators are responsible for reporting and interpreting the results of student assessment, especially standardized test scores, to school trustees and to the larger community. These reports require careful planning on the administrators' part because they must be accurate in terms of the data and its interpretation, but they must also be couched in terms noneducators can understand.

We believe the most useful approach to such reports is to begin, not with the test statistics for a school or district, but by asking, "What questions do my parents, the community, and the news media want answered?" Determine what these audiences most want to learn, formulate questions, prepare answers, then back up the responses with data from the state or testing company's reports.

For example: at a meeting with parents, an administrator may be asked, "On the state examinations, are our middle school students showing good progress in reading?" The response might be, "Yes, in each of our middle school grades on our statewide tests, average scores in reading equal or exceed the state norms." If more details are desired, an administrator can be prepared to break out the reading scores by grade, school, and by achievement levels (top, medium, and low-scoring cohorts); the administrator can then compare them with previous years' scores and with districts/schools with comparable demographics, but these data can become an overwhelming amount of information for laymen to digest. Educators in the system and school board members should review the follow-up information mentioned in the previous sentence, and teachers should be given the time and the training to understand their own students' scores in relation to the test content and norms.

A STUDENT REPORT

There is no single best format for report cards, periodic reports of students' progress. The report in figure 12.1 represents a reasonably complete summary of a student's progress in middle school mathematics, and one that also enables a teacher to complete the form quickly.

Some teachers and administrators will find the suggested report form insufficiently detailed. If parents and student received no other feedback, the suggested form would indeed be inadequate. As recommended earlier, details of student performance—test results, graded homework, teacher

Figure 12.1. Report Card

Fremont Middle School
Midville, California
Report for Marking Period
September 1–October 31, 2007

Student's Name: Henrietta Higgins   Grade Level: Eight
Subject: Mathematics   Teacher: A. Lehrer
Subject Grade: E   Effort Grade: E
    Grade Symbols: E = Excellent, S = Satisfactory
    N = Needs Improvement, U = Unsatisfactory

    Important Knowledge and Skills in Mathematics
Knows Basic Facts   Computes Accurately
Understands Concepts   Uses Calculator/Computer Accurately
Uses Problem-Solving Skills Accurately

    Principal Bases for Student's Grade
Results of Classroom Assessment: Major Tests, Oral and Written Quizzes
Contributions to Classroom Discussions
Homework

---

observations—should be provided continuously throughout a grading period. Such information is timely and can be as detailed as is appropriate to
the student's performance. The periodic grade report then becomes simply
a summary of information that all parties have already shared. As much as
possible, information in the first section should be preprinted, with each
teacher filling in the remaining information.

We do not suggest creating parental expectations by labeling a final section, Comments. If the form in figure 12.1 were printed on a standard 8½
× 11 page, a teacher would have ample space to add a brief message, such
as, "Please call me for an appointment."

Note the separate grade for Effort. This item could be construed to include classroom behavior; a low grade would call for a discussion with parents of specific concerns and what parents, teacher, and student will do to
remedy them.

The range of symbols, E, S, N, and U, should be discussed in faculty meetings and agreement reached on descriptions and weightings of each symbol. An obvious example would be a student who is strong in all three of
the Principal Bases would receive an Excellent rating; a student whose classroom assessment results and class contributions are very strong, but whose
homework is just satisfactory could probably still be rated Excellent. One
with satisfactory ratings on class participation and homework, but high
grades on classroom assessment might receive an overall grade of Satisfactory. But these are judgment calls, which is why faculty members need to
discuss them and reach some general agreement on them.

Percentages or other more detailed scoring rubrics are useful for grading
tests, but can convey a false precision when used in a summative grade report. We've heard of high schools in which a student with a grade point average (GPA) of 99.22 is recognized as "better" than a student with a GPA of
99.16. There is, of course, no significant difference between these grades,
and it's certain that the assessments that contribute to the grades have some
margins of error. No doubt, each of the two students has academic strengths
and weaknesses the other does not, but these differences cannot be expressed by narrowly differing percentages.

It's true that tests in certain subjects like mathematics or spelling lend
themselves to specific, even exact scores. But most teachers find it difficult
to explain the difference in student learning represented by a score of 88
percent versus 91 percent, or a grade of A compared with a B+. This is most
obviously true in assessments like essays or classroom observations that
don't lend themselves to simple counting.

Teachers and parents need to remind themselves that grades are *estimates*,
approximations that represent the best judgment of one or more teachers
about a student's academic achievement. Test scores and grades are snap-
shots of a student's performance at specific times, while student achieve-

ment is typically uneven, with learning spurts and occasional regressions comprising a normal part of children's development.

Finally, in the interests of good record-keeping and saving teachers' time, we recommend they consider using computer grade books. This relatively inexpensive software allows calculation of averages with weightings of various measures and other statistics. Printouts can be a useful adjunct to parent conferences.

SUMMARY

- Students and parents should be made aware of all elements that contribute to the grading process.
- Parents can expect to be informed promptly of any serious problem or deficiency in their children's behavior or academic progress.
- Parents should be routinely informed of their children's academic progress during a grading period by seeing teachers' grades and comments on homework, periodic tests, and projects.
- Teachers should immediately report to administrators and parents any serious concerns about their students' academic progress or behavior.
- Routine periodic reports should be brief summaries that contain no surprises for students or their parents.
- School administrators have a several responsibilities for assessment: to monitor grades assigned by teachers, to support teachers through providing in-service training and mediating controversies with parents over grades, and to report assessment results to the board and community.

V

PROGRAM EVALUATION AND ACCOUNTABILITY

In this part, we examine two complementary topics. Program evaluation justifies or systematically plans revisions in school programs. Accountability refers more generally to the schools' obligations of setting goals, assessing how well they are achieved, and reporting the results to the many parties who have a stake in the outcomes of schooling.

Chapter 13 examines why evaluating their curriculum is so important for teachers, administrators, and school trustees. We then describe the process of conducting both small-scale and more significant evaluations.

Chapter 14 speaks first to the reasons schools must hold themselves accountable. We review the complex research and its sometimes ambiguous conclusions about using student test results to measure teachers' contribution to student achievement. The chapter concludes by examining two basic responsibilities for which schools must be accountable: good teaching and, with some limitations, students' academic progress.

13

Program Evaluation

THE RATIONALE FOR PROGRAM EVALUATION

When we *assess* a performance or program, we gather data and organize it into systematic categories, then summarize the results. When we *evaluate*, we analyze and reflect on the data, draw inferences, and make judgments or decisions based on what the data tell us. When a teachers wants to determine the merits of some element in her curriculum, or consider adding a topic, a resource, or a teaching methodology to the curriculum, she first gathers data and interprets it; then she forms a judgment and makes a decision.

WHY IS PROGRAM EVALUATION IMPORTANT FOR TEACHERS?

Program evaluation is a commonsense part of teaching and school administration. The various curricula from kindergarten through twelfth grade include a multitude of elements in terms of content and teaching methodology. What works well? Would an alternative approach work better? How can students in a given class or an entire district be better assisted to learn, given the resources available? These are obvious questions for school professionals to pose, but answering such queries and undertaking the tasks they imply compete with many other priorities. It's only too easy to fall into "curriculum inertia." "I teach this unit or use these texts because that's how I've always taught the course." "I use a constructivist approach with my classes because that's what my preparation program trained me to do."

The relationship of student assessment and curriculum evaluation is illustrated in the recent findings on student literacy by the National Assessment of Educational Progress (Tomsho, 2007). High schools report that their students are taking more courses of greater rigor in English than in prior years. Yet test scores show a general decline in reading, especially in reading for literary experience, which includes plot, character development, and other elements vital to understanding a literary work. So, assessment reveals a counterintuitive result: As students are taking more and more demanding courses in English, their achievement as measured by test scores in important elements of the subject is declining.

In dealing with this issue, schools could examine a number of possible explanations. An obvious concern is whether the newer standards and the English literature curricula based on them are congruent with test specifications. Teachers and administrators would have to compare NAEP specifications and actual tests with their curricula; if they find substantial discrepancies, they must decide whether to modify their curricula or accept the lower scores that follow when students have not been taught significant knowledge and skills that are measured by the tests.

A second possible explanation is that students are not reading beyond their classroom, and aren't being challenged and pushed in class to exercise critical-thinking skills like analysis and evaluation of the assigned reading.

Whatever the source of the apparent anomaly of more courses but lower achievement, the importance of evaluating the effectiveness of content and teaching methods in high school English is highlighted by results from student assessment. Answering the questions "Does it work?" or "Is this the best content; are these the best teaching methods for my students?" can set the questioner on a path that requires at least a little effort, sometimes a lot. How teachers and administrators can answer these questions efficiently and effectively is our topic in this chapter.

THE PROCESS OF PROGRAM EVALUATION

Three Questions

Every element of the curriculum should be reviewed periodically. Begin with these three questions:

One, is this program demonstrably *effective?* That is, do the results meet our objectives in terms of student knowledge, skills, and other desired outcomes?

Two, is the program *worth the cost?* If only time and money were not constraints! But they are; does this program provide benefits in proportion to the costs?

Three, is the program *acceptable* to all parties of interest? The board likes the program, but the teachers think it's badly flawed; teachers and administrators are enthusiastic, but students and parents are bewildered. If a school program does not enjoy general acceptance, or at least a neutral, wait-and-see attitude on the part of all key players in a school, either the opinions or the program should be changed.

SMALL-SCALE EVALUATIONS

We said that the process of reviewing and making decisions about elements of a curriculum may require a little effort, or even quite a bit of effort. Let's begin with an example of a "little effort."

In his eleventh grade literature class, Mr. Parker wants to try out a small change in his usual teaching strategy by asking each student to choose and read aloud some favorite lines of dialogue from *Romeo and Juliet*; students are to say why they like the lines, and what they tell them about the characters who speak them. Mr. Parker's purpose is to move his students to read the play slowly and carefully, to select especially meaningful lines and passages, and to reflect aloud on what the words say about the qualities and motivations of the speakers. The teacher encourages other students to comment, ask questions, and make connections with other characters and plot actions. The teacher's larger intent is to improve his students' knowledge, understanding, and appreciation of a Shakespearean masterwork.

How should Mr. Parker evaluate the success of his proposed instructional strategy? His principal source of assessment is built into the new teaching technique. That is, as he listens to the passages his students have chosen, and their explanations for choosing them, he can assess the extent to which this approach has improved his students' engagement with the text. Have they learned more, understood better, appreciated more deeply than when other teaching strategies were employed? Of course, Mr. Parker may choose to give a written test that assesses the same questions, but he will almost surely learn more from his observations and interactions with his students. He can then make a decision on incorporating the new technique into his teaching repertoire.

Experienced teachers will recognize that this simple example could be improved by a few other considerations, such as, "Does the new technique take up an unrealistic amount of class time?" "Do the students respond well to the new approach?" And even, "How do I factor students' responses into their final grade?" Still, Mr. Parker's strategy for determining the worth of his new teaching technique has the elements of good program evaluation. He knows what he wants to accomplish and how his instructional method fits with the overall purpose of his course. His criterion is student learning.

His plan and use of observation to measure the effectiveness of the new technique are appropriate, and sufficient to drive a decision about adding the new approach to his battery of teaching methods.

LESS SIMPLE EVALUATIONS

Now let's consider how to evaluate a somewhat more complex example, a program that requires more effort and carries greater consequences for instruction.

Ms. Sayers teaches ninth and tenth grade Latin classes; her students learn vocabulary and grammar from their texts and apply their knowledge to reading selections from Caesar and Cicero. Ms. Sayers defends her traditional emphasis on declensions, conjugations, and memorizing Latin vocabulary as critical building blocks in preparing her students to read Latin poetry in grades eleven and twelve. Her principal tells Ms. Sayers that he hears complaints that her Latin course is too difficult and requires a disproportionate amount of student preparation time. He suggests a more relaxed approach, including reading the Latin authors in English translations.

How should Ms. Sayers's Latin course be evaluated?

1. The starting point for every program evaluation is to ask, "what are the *objectives* of the course?" Ms. Sayers's primary purpose is to prepare her ninth and tenth graders for the demands of third and fourth year Latin. Her secondary objectives are to enhance students' abilities in reading and writing English by emphasizing the Latinate foundations of English, and to familiarize her students with the importance of grammar and the richness of classical literature.

   Note that the principal's objectives differ in important respects from those of the teacher. Those who will make judgments based on the results of an evaluation must first agree on the objectives of the program; otherwise there is little point in proceeding with an evaluation.
2. How will results of an evaluation be *used?* In this case, will a decision follow to modify the course content or teaching approaches? If results are negative or ambiguous, will the principal's suggested approach be implemented?
3. What's the *plan?* How will the evaluators determine whether the course objectives have been achieved at satisfactory levels? Who will conduct the evaluation? When will data be gathered? When can a report and recommendations be expected? Who will make a decision?
4. What *assessment instruments and techniques* are best suited to gathering the needed data? The Latin course evaluator would start with the first objective and ask, "How successful are Ms. Sayers's students in third

and fourth year Latin?" The grades they receive from their teachers in advanced courses are a good indicator. If many students in senior Latin receive 3s, 4s, or 5s on the Advanced Placement Latin examinations, that's also powerful evidence of good preparation. What do upper-level students say about how well they are prepared for the rigors of third and fourth year Latin?

What about another of Ms. Sayers's objectives, to improve students' abilities in reading and writing English? One assessment technique would involve preparing a set of questions for experienced English teachers in the school. The teachers would be asked to compare their students who have taken Ms. Sayers's Latin class with those who have not. The general intent of improving students' reading and writing skills would be broken into specific questions, for example, Are the Latin students better able to recognize or to reason out the meaning of English terms? Do they use a richer, more varied vocabulary in their writing than students who have not taken two years of Latin?

These simple assessment techniques, using later course grades or collegial opinions to assess the achievement of course objectives, are not perfect. They are open to questions like: "Does the advantage attributed to Latin students constitute statistically significant gains?" "Are the Latin students a select group who might have done better in later English classes even if they had not taken Ms. Sayers's Latin courses?" "How do we know that the instructional strategies suggested by the principal would not have resulted in equal gains?" These are fair questions; the teacher and principal may want to initiate more formal studies and statistical treatments to respond to them and other possible questions.

In accord with our intent for this text, we urge teachers and administrators to use assessment processes that are simple and straightforward, even if they lack ideal evidence of validity and reliability. We take this position not out of disdain for well-designed studies, but from our own school experience. Complex curriculum assessment does indeed yield more reliable results, but in most schools and classrooms, such studies will not be undertaken: It is better to evaluate less than perfectly than not to evaluate at all.

5. The role of *expert judgment*: What works for other teachers? In this example, our principal should realize his limitations in prescribing changes in a teacher's curriculum. Assuming his degree is not in classics, or even if it is, he should seek advice from experienced Latin teachers who teach in schools similar to his own. Teachers trust the real world in which their colleagues live. If a program works well for other teachers, and students in their schools are reasonably similar to those in one's own school, considerable weight should be given to the experiences of colleagues in other schools.

6. Having gathered data, the next step is to *analyze* them, that is, look at the results and ask, "What do they mean?" In our example, the person conducting the investigation—probably not Ms. Sayers, who has a personal interest in the outcome—looks at the impressions and opinions of the English teachers concerning the value of early Latin study. If four respondents say that students with Latin preparation are "substantially better" in their writing and speaking vocabulary than their peers, and one says "I see no difference," the investigator may reasonably conclude that one of Ms. Sayers's objectives appears to be met.

   Again, the upper-division teachers' opinions are somewhat "soft" data, so evaluations based on them must be less than dogmatic. But it is a relatively easy way to gather and evaluate some information that is based on student learning. Such a process also contributes to instruction, as the literature teachers reflect on the preparation of their students that seems to contribute to their success in reading and writing.

7. *Recommendations and decisions* follow evaluations. After those responsible for evaluating Ms. Sayers's Latin I and II courses offer recommendations consistent with their evaluation, the decision maker, presumably the principal, should discuss the results and recommendations of the investigation with Ms. Sayers. If the recommendations are contrary to the teacher's current organization of her courses, she should have an opportunity to comment or offer a rebuttal. But all parties have known, from the beginning of the evaluation, that a decision must be made, and that it will be based on the study's findings. Ms. Sayers may not agree with the outcome, but she cannot argue that the process of reaching a decision was arbitrary or unfair.

BIGGER AND BETTER EVALUATIONS

If the preceding paragraphs seem to encourage program evaluation procedures that are less than rigorous, that's just what they're meant to do. Teachers should question every element of their courses: "Could I add or substitute a set of assignments, a text, or a teaching methodology that might make my course more interesting and productive of learning for my students?" Good teachers constantly look for more effective content and teaching methods; this ongoing tinkering with their lesson plans makes for steady improvement in student participation and growth, and makes classes more interesting for teachers. We strongly support such attempts to improve teaching; we simply urge that the proposed improvements be subjected to *some* scrutiny, that is, assessment and evaluation, concerning their effectiveness. But for program evaluations like those just described, the perfect is the enemy of the good. A less-than-comprehensive assessment and evaluation can yield useful information; a more complex process would not be completed.

Not all proposed changes in schools are little ones. If the Minneapolis public school system wants to consider changing its approach to teaching reading in the primary grades to a scripted reading approach, or the Albuquerque schools are being urged to switch their K–12 curriculum to the Singapore Math program, a full-scale, carefully planned assessment and evaluation process is called for. For such critical curriculum issues, decision makers need an evaluation study that includes the most valid and reliable measures that are available. The budget for such a study will call for substantial funding and many days of professional efforts, from initial planning to final recommendations, and reports may take months to complete. Is such an expensive, time-consuming effort worth it? Absolutely! Proposals for major curriculum changes deserve painstaking review and study because the decisions that flow from them can affect thousands of students over many years.

The principal conditions for such a major program evaluation are: First, it's a high-stakes issue, that is, significant changes are being proposed that will influence many students and teachers across schools and school years. Second, resources—the funds and professional time to conduct the study and to implement results must be available. Third, transparency—all parties of interest, especially teachers and including parents, should be kept informed of the purpose of the evaluation, who will conduct it, and how, and be given an opportunity to comment on the initial findings and the final report.

Classroom teachers will surely be involved in such major evaluations, but studies of this magnitude are best organized and conducted by specialists with expertise in assessing and evaluating large-scale school programs. We make this recommendation because an external evaluator will usually bring a degree of competence, commitment, and objectivity that are difficult for internal staff to match.

The process for conducting a full-scale program evaluation is basically the same set of steps that is described for Ms. Sayers's Latin program; those steps determine:

1. The objectives of the evaluation
2. How the results will be used
3. The evaluation plan
4. The assessment instruments
5. The role of expert judgment
6. Data gathering and analysis

7. The reporting process
8. The decision process

PRELIMINARY DECISIONS

Trustees, administrators, and teachers should agree on two basic decisions as they consider initiating a formal, complex program evaluation.

First, the school or district should spell out—literally, in writing—*why* the evaluation is important. Such a statement will include the purposes of the study, separated into measurable objectives, what the final report should contain, and how the results of the evaluation will be used. This statement is critically important to reaching agreement with the evaluators and to avoiding misunderstandings and disappointments with the study results. This formal procedure is sometimes omitted because "everyone understands this program and knows why we should evaluate it." Formulating a rationale for the evaluation forces a board or faculty to agree on why the evaluation is important, but also requires a revisiting of the objectives of the program itself, and what they expect it to accomplish.

Second, *who* is in charge, that is, who in the school system is authorized to make decisions, approve expenditures, monitor the schedule and budget, submit interim reports, and so on. This official must have the time and skills to interact with outside evaluators and to communicate to trustees and administrators the progress of the study and any problems it encounters. This role of the school district's own monitor is critical to any investigation carried out by external investigators. Costly program research projects can result in disappointment and a failure to act on the project's recommendations; usually, these expensive failures could have been avoided by careful oversight, consultation, and reporting during the course of the project.

The evaluation plan with a description of the design and sampling, selection and/or development of assessment instruments, data collection and analyses processes is primarily the responsibility of the professional evaluators. If the study authorizers have done their preliminary work well, and the study process is monitored appropriately, the study report and recommended applications of results should prove convincing and useful to those who authorized the study. We recommend that administrators and board members who contemplate such a major study begin by familiarizing themselves with the complexities of large-scale program evaluation. They can start by consulting the American Educational Research Association's website (2007), or the ERIC Clearinghouse on Assessment and Evaluation (Capps, n.d.). They will also find useful the *AEA Guiding Principles Training Package,* published by the American Evaluation Association (n.d.).

SUMMARY

- To evaluate a program is to analyze and make judgments about it based on the results of assessment.
- Teachers constantly evaluate the content of their courses and methods of presenting it. Most often such evaluation is informal, but can easily be made somewhat more systematic, thereby increasing its reliability and usefulness.
- Three key questions to pose in reviewing a program are: First, does the program achieve its intended outcomes? Second, is the program cost-effective? Third, is the program acceptable to all parties of interest?
- Teachers can plan an evaluation that asks, first, what are the program's objectives? Second, how will the results of the evaluation will be used? Third, what are the appropriate assessment instruments and techniques? Fourth, what are the experiences of other teachers? Fifth, how will the assessment data be analyzed and integrated? And sixth, what decisions on retaining or changing the program will follow the evaluation?
- Major systemwide decisions on educational programs call for substantial commitment of time and money; these large-scale evaluations are best conducted by experts from outside the school system.

14

Accountability

THE NATURE OF AND REASONS
FOR SCHOOL ACCOUNTABILITY

A Three-Step Process

What characterizes a school that holds itself accountable? Such a school:

Adopts measurable objectives;
Assesses its success in achieving its objectives; and
Reports the results of its assessments to students, parents, and the community.

The Reasons for School Accountability

Perhaps we are belaboring the obvious, but let's look at *why* a school should be accountable, understanding that "school" is shorthand for trustees, administrators, teachers, and support staff.

Accountability is required of those who are doing something important; the greater the impact of their actions, the more accountable they are, and that is true of both institutions and individuals. Governmental bodies like legislatures or corporations like Intel are expected to report to those who support them and are affected by their actions. Individual leaders of government are substantially responsible for the welfare of their constituents, so voters hold them accountable, and periodically demand that they show the extent to which they have achieved their objectives and justified the trust that has been put in them. The willingness to be held accountable is, in government, one of the obvious distinctions between democracies and dictatorships.

In general, our economic system runs on accountability; if a company fails to show a profit, the marketplace will hold it accountable and it will eventually fail. Nonprofit organizations like public schools do not have financial gain as an objective, so they are assessed on other criteria. The critical requisite for accountability is a clear set of expectations; these are objectives that an institution has agreed to achieve, or to make reasonable progress toward achieving. Our primary expectation for schools is that their students will acquire the knowledge, skills, and attitudes that will enable them to continue learning and to live productive lives. The primary responsibility for achieving that learning devolves on the trustees, administrators, and teachers in the schools.

When we hold school boards and education professionals accountable for student learning, we should be measuring effectiveness primarily by the results of schooling, not the resources placed in the schools. The amount of per-pupil spending, the number of books in school libraries, even the certification or seniority of teachers are inputs to schooling, not outcomes. As long as inputs can be correlated with important student needs, they are appropriate means to an end.

TEACHERS' ACCOUNTABILITY FOR STUDENT LEARNING

We said earlier that student test results should be used carefully and only as partial measures of effective teaching. (See chapter 8, Using the Results of Standardized Tests.) Yet the use of student test results as the *sole* measure of schools' or teachers' effectiveness is increasingly common in state testing programs. So we'll add a few comments on that topic.

Begin with what common sense and research studies show—teachers can and do have an effect on their students' learning. However, the magnitude of the effect, that is, *how much* of student learning is due to the teaching they receive, is less clear.

When we use student test scores to measure the impact of teachers on student learning, the outcomes are modified by various factors: the effects of other in- and out-of-school influences, the number of students in the classes, their preparation and achievement level, the curriculum taught versus the content of the test, and sampling error in the test instruments. All of these factors should be weighed when we look for causes of students' achievement.

Another way of considering student test scores as measures of teacher effectiveness is to respond to two questions: Can teachers affect student learning? Yes. Can the learning attributable to teachers be measured by standardized tests? The most careful and accurate response seems to be "yes," but only sometimes and partially. As is usually the case when a simple or single measure is used to assess a complex phenomenon, results of student testing can contribute only crude measures of teacher effectiveness.

A teacher whose students' test scores consistently and significantly outpace those of other, comparable students can reasonably be considered an excellent teacher. Of course, the converse is equally probable; a teacher whose students show consistently poor achievement when compared with similar students is surely not excellent, and probably not even adequate. "Consistently" means over a period of time and with numerous classes. "Significantly" reminds us that small gains or losses cannot be reliable bases for evaluation. Judgments at the extremes of teacher performance—the outstanding or the manifestly incompetent—will usually be confirmed by students' achievement results. In these cases, students' assessment scores simply confirm what principals and other teachers already know, but they may be useful to document rewards or sanctions.

However, student test scores don't tell us much that is useful about teachers whose students fall in the very broad middle range of test results, those who neither greatly exceed nor fall notably below reasonable expectations. Certainly, student test results alone do not permit reliable ranking of all teachers in a school or district by their teaching ability.

A number of recent research studies contribute to this issue of value-added measures of teacher effectiveness. See especially the Rand study by Daniel F. McCaffrey and colleagues (2004), a paper by Henry Braun (2000) that lays out the promise and problems of value-added measures and is especially useful for educational laymen, and *Evaluating Value-Added: Findings and Recommendations from the NASBE Study Group on Value-Added Models* (National Association of State Boards of Education, 2005). The commission concludes that value-added assessment is not designed for high-stakes testing in teacher evaluation. Its second finding, however, is that value-added assessment has significant potential, when used in conjunction with other measures, as a tool for improving teaching.

We believe that the first finding is too sweeping, but it appears to be modified by the second statement, with which we agree. These findings of the National Association of State Boards of Education (NASBE, 2005) seem inconsistent with state boards' use of results of state-mandated tests to determine teacher effectiveness, as the NCLB demands. The state boards and departments of education apparently do not use "other measures and supports" to determine teachers' and schools' effectiveness, as the NASBE urges.

Another important and complex study of the relationship between teacher competence and student learning is the Tennessee Value-Added Assessment System, devised by William A. Sanders. The results attempt to link student performance on tests with individual teachers, supporting Sanders' theory that teacher effectiveness is the most important factor in predicting student academic growth (Project STAR, 1999).

A frequently cited objection to using student gain scores to measure teachers' effectiveness is that they do not measure certain important elements of student learning. That assertion is accurate; achievement test scores tell us nothing about students' growth in physical, emotional, or social skills. Test scores can only give us information about students' progress in one goal of schooling: academic achievement. But that information is *enormously important* because it references the fundamental goal of schooling. As noted earlier, teaching students to read, write, calculate, and gain the other knowledge and skills embraced in an academic curriculum is the purpose that schools are best able to achieve. Academic learning is what communities expect of their schools; when classes of children do not master basic skills and subject matter, schools have failed; a failure of a school will, in large part, be deemed a failure of teachers and administrators.

What can schools use as additional accountability measures to demonstrate teacher competence? An obvious and common basis for such judgments is supervisory observation of classroom teaching and its effects on students. Students' enjoyment and learning from interactions with their teachers, plus other observable teacher activities that contribute to student learning or other school goals, are all measures of effective teaching. Obviously, the observer must be capable of interpreting student reactions, their linkages with the various styles of good teaching, and the many elements that contribute to an effective school.

It's beyond the scope of this book to address how supervisors should assess and evaluate teaching practices and use the results of those evaluations to improve classroom instruction. Because the process relies so much on professional judgment, it's easy to quarrel with some supervisors' evaluations of their staff. But the evaluation of performance by one's supervisor is the commonest form of performance appraisal in most areas of business and other professions. Are supervisors sometimes insufficiently skilled in the qualities they are observing? Can they be biased in favor of or against certain teachers whom they evaluate? Of course they can.

But most principals and supervisors are both competent and fair. That a few are neither is reason for an appeals process, and for using multiple measures of teaching effectiveness. The solution, which will never work perfectly, is to use several measures, more than one observer, and constantly seek to improve all elements of the evaluation process. It's tempting to rely solely on the seeming precision of student gain scores. When the scores are from a single assessment, when the gains are small, or when test results are not supplemented by other performance variables, judgments about teachers' effectiveness are of questionable validity.

REPORTING RESPONSIBILITIES

Schools that hold themselves accountable to students and parents for academic achievement provide two types of information. The first is the extent to which students have mastered a subject in relation to the criteria set out in the course objectives. Call this *criterion-referenced reporting*. Students and parents have a right to know how well students have achieved the major learning objectives in a course, so a commitment to accountability obliges schools to report that information.

A second kind of reporting should accompany criterion-referenced reports. These reports answer the question, "To what extent have other students of the same age/grade mastered the same objectives?" In addition to reporting achievement on the basis of learning criteria, schools should compare individual and groups of students with norms, that is, with the grades and scores of comparable groups of students. This *norm-referenced reporting* is also critical to understanding student achievement. Consider the quality of information in the following notes sent to parents by eighth grade English teachers:

"John's A in his writing project places him in the top 20 percent of students in his class. He has mastered the five-paragraph essay, and has made a good start in developing his own prose style."
"Mary participates enthusiastically in our writing assignments. She contributes to class discussions, and accepts directions well."

We learn that, in the teacher's judgment, John is writing well in relation to his classmates and to several important objectives in his writing course. How well his class as a whole writes is also important if John and his parents are to form a clear picture of his skills. When results on a standardized test of writing allow John and his class to be compared with some larger norm, students and parents learn still more about the quality of John's writing.

Mary's parents will no doubt be pleased to learn of their daughter's enthusiasm, but they have learned nothing about her writing skills, or where she stands in relation to others in her class, or to any other sample of her peers. Let's assume that one objective of John's and Mary's school is, "Students will demonstrate clear and effective writing skills." However, Mary's school has not accounted to her parents for how well she achieved that objective. But it may also be true that "clear and effective writing skills" is not an objective of Mary's school, or the school has not defined what evidence demonstrates effective writing.

As recommended in chapter 12, Reporting Results of Assessment, these formal reports should be brief and not anecdotal. Teachers' comments like

those exemplified in the previous example are intended to supplement a
graded test or project.

WHAT ARE SCHOOLS ACCOUNTABLE FOR?

Schools are accountable for doing what they promise to do. If parents are
told, "By the end of first grade, every child will be reading," or, "At least 80
percent of our graduating seniors will be admitted to college," teachers in
first grade, or principals, counselors, and teachers in high school must ensure that these results are achieved, or explain credibly why they are not. At
a parents' association meeting, a principal may state, "By the end of this
school year, the average of our sixth graders' reading scores will match the
national average." In some schools that would be a tremendously ambi-
tious goal, in others it would be setting the bar pretty low.

Some minimal objectives should be common to all schools. By the end
of grade three, for example, virtually all children should be able to read,
speak, and write simple but correct English, and to solve problems in basic
arithmetic. Every high school should set a yearly "graduation objective,"
and have a plan that gradually reduces the school's dropout rate. We speak
of "virtually all children" and "gradually reduce" because in goals for
school improvement as in other areas of life, the perfect can be the enemy
of the good. Factors beyond the schools' control can make 100 percent
achievement of a goal impossible. Isolated exceptions should not be allowed to brand a school or a class a "failure."

The No Child Left Behind Act says that all public school systems must report annually on the following categories:

1. Academic achievement by all student groups
2. A comparison of basic, proficient, and advanced proficient students in
   school districts and nationwide
3. High school graduation and dropout rates
4. Professional qualifications of teachers
5. Percentages of students not tested
6. Schools "in need of improvement"

Unfortunately, the NCLB lost much of its credibility among educators by
requiring that "All students will . . . ." Reminding us of our obligation to the
least privileged and often neglected children is admirable, but a goal of 100
percent achievement is simply unachievable. It is true that teachers and
schools are responsible for each individual student, but that obligation
does not translate into accountability for ensuring that every student learns
all that he needs to learn; such a demand cannot be satisfied. Teachers are

obliged to be prepared to teach, to follow good practices of their profession, and to do all they can to help each student achieve. But teachers cannot properly be held accountable for every desired result for every student because they cannot control all the variables that determine learning.

What then can we expect teachers to be accountable for in relation to their students' academic achievement?

First, *good teaching*. The two most obvious requisites for good teachers are solid knowledge and skills in their subject, and a repertoire of teaching strategies. Applying these qualities in the classroom means following a prescribed curriculum in which the content is coherent from unit to unit and grade to grade, and adjusting teaching methods to the needs of a class and, insofar as possible, to the needs of each student. A teacher who substitutes his own course for the one that the state and district have mandated, who fails to maintain a pace that ensures that the prescribed material will be taught and the objectives met, or who does not adjust his teaching methods to his students' strengths and weaknesses, is professionally irresponsible; his students will be handicapped in their ensuing courses, as well as in taking examinations based on the approved curriculum.

That last phrase sounds as if we are advocating "teaching to the test." Not so: We encourage teaching to the standards and curriculum guidelines on which tests, especially state tests, are based. Or consider programs like the Advanced Placement (AP) or International Baccalaureate (IB) curricula. They are densely packed courses, based on carefully developed standards and learning objectives. If students in these classes are to take the programs' examinations, teachers must follow the curricula very closely. If "teaching to the test" means focusing preparation on the standards and objectives on which tests are based so that students can be prepared to do well on the test, then we are in favor of teaching to the test. If it means drilling on test items, we oppose it.

A formal curriculum should include the essential outcomes of a course and any resources necessary to achieve them. Such a curriculum should allow teachers to decide on appropriate schedules, teaching techniques, and the like. Ideally, state-prescribed objectives should focus on critical outcomes, leaving teachers free to provide additional topics they select. Unfortunately, most state curriculum standards seem to include virtually everything every member of the standards development committee considers desirable, leaving little time for teachers' initiatives and favorite topics. The same is largely true for AP and IB courses. If students plan to take the national exams in these programs, teachers are left with few curriculum choices.

Similarly, a teacher is obliged to adjust her teaching to the strengths and weaknesses of the students in her class. In chapter 1 we speak of the differing styles of teaching that various students need. Professional teachers are not restricted to a single style of teaching; they have a range of skills to match the readiness of their students to learn.

Second, we expect *student learning*. If teachers have strong preparation in their subjects, and a repertoire of skills that can be adjusted to student needs, the great majority of students will learn in their classes. But what if teachers lack either of these qualities, if school authorities (and parents) do not require student behavior that is adequate for learning, or if the curriculum lacks coherence and is not based on proven principles of learning? Under these circumstances many, even most students, will not learn, and schools can be held accountable for the failure. For all the criticism of the NCLB, it is a right-directed demand for accountability that underlies the Act's insistence on setting learning goals and assessing their achievement.

For how much student learning should schools be accountable? First, for achieving explicitly defined, basic information and skills in each course, and second, for showing year-to-year progress. This standard applies to the great majority of students, and NCLB rightly insists on breaking out class averages by certain traditionally underserved subgroups. But the realistic goal cannot be that each child will make "adequate progress" every year. Most students don't progress on a smooth, upward curve every year, and a few students may fail to grasp the fundamentals of a course despite their teachers' best efforts. Class averages can be expected to register fairly consistent progress, while subgroups in a class will vary somewhat in yearly achievement. Individual students may progress rapidly one year, then plateau or even regress the following year on standardized achievement measures. These conditions may reflect important events in a student's life outside of school, or simply show an uneven, but normal pattern of development over a period of years.

This book is primarily directed to teachers, but they know well that they cannot be held solely accountable for all student achievement. Teachers are like pediatricians who use their superior knowledge of children's health and development to diagnose, prescribe, and monitor their young patients. Children's doctors bear a considerable responsibility for the well-being of their young charges. When a child is hospitalized, the institution also becomes responsible for providing care at an acceptable professional level. These responsibilities are somewhat analogous to those of a teacher and a school.

Parents also have a substantial obligation in relation to their children's health. If children are exposed to the risk of disease or injury at home, if they do not receive adequate affection, nourishment, or sleep, their doctors can try to remedy the effects of such neglect, but it's a difficult and often losing struggle. Teachers and schools can strive to offset the effects of a home environment that is inimical to study and learning, but the effort is demanding in terms of resources. Only schools and teachers with the goals, curricula, resources, and training that such an effort demands can hope to succeed in the face of an inadequate home environment.

Nor should we overlook the obligation of the students themselves. Especially as students in middle and high school push for greater independence, they should constantly be reminded that, with freedom, comes responsibility. They share accountability for their own welfare and learning. Woody Allen is quoted as saying that "Ninety percent of a job is showing up." A student's primary obligation is to attend class; teachers can't do much with empty desks. A major reason for student dropouts in high school is that some students lose the thread of instruction because they have missed classes. If their deficiencies are not remedied, they become bored and restless when they return to class because the gaps in their learning render them unable to make sense of the instruction.

SUMMARY

- The accountable school:

  Adopts measurable objectives;
  Assesses its students' achievement of the objectives; and
  Reports the results of its assessment to students, parents, and the community.

- Student test results can contribute an important but partial measure of teachers' performance.
- Accountability calls for two types of reporting: on the criteria of students' mastery of the course objectives, and on students' performance in relation to their peers.
- Teachers are accountable for knowledge of their subjects and appropriate teaching strategies. They are also responsible in part for student learning, that is, for students achieving basic course objectives and demonstrating progress over time.
- Parents and students are also accountable for students' learning. Teachers and schools can only succeed with parents' support and students' efforts.

Glossary

accountability means the complete and accurate reporting of goals, procedures, and assessment results.

achievement tests measure the extent to which a test-taker has acquired a body of knowledge and skills.

analytic scoring assigns subscores to components of an assessment. An overall score on a writing test, for example, might include distinct scores for style, spelling, punctuation, and so on.

anecdotal record refers to a description of some performance or activity; it should include circumstances that influence the performance, and should interpret or score the performance.

aptitude test refers to a measure purporting to predict an ability to learn certain knowledge or skills.

assessment is the gathering of data to measure performance.

authentic assessment means the use of some observable and measurable performance as evidence of learning.

average score is the sum of all scores divided by the number of scores; also termed the *mean.*

behavioral objectives state the performance to be measured, the conditions of the performance, and the level required for mastery.

classroom assessments are the various forms of assessment chosen and used by classroom teachers.

correlation coefficient is a statistic describing the relationship between two sets of measures. There is, for example, a positive but not perfect correlation between height and weight, or scores on IQ and achievement tests.

criterion-referenced assessment measures the degree of mastery of a given body of knowledge or skills.

efficiency means the balance between the time and effort required to devise, administer, and score assessments, and the adequate sampling or representation of the domain being tested.

equivalent forms refers to alternative tests that are equal in difficulty.

evaluation signifies a judgment based on the results of assessment.

formative evaluation uses assessment results for giving advice and support, rather than summarizing or making decisions about overall performance.

free-response items signifies questions or problems that require test-takers to generate their own responses rather than choose from a given set of options.

grade-equivalent scores show the average levels of performance at every grade level. A grade-equivalent score of 5.4 is the level expected of an average student in the fourth month of grade five.

holistic scoring refers to assigning a score on some measure based on an overall impression, rather that an analysis of components. To obtain acceptable reliability, scorers using this method must receive training, practice, and monitoring.

independent norms indicate the level of performance of a sample of students in independent schools.

item analysis provides each student's responses to every question on a test; it also gives the correct answer and how many students in a class chose it, as well as the number of students who chose each incorrect response.

learning disability refers to a quality in an individual that interferes with the ability to learn through normal methods of instruction.

local norms represent the performance of a specific class, school, or school system.

mastery testing considers the extent to which a student has achieved specific learning objectives that are designated as a standard of proficiency.

mean score is the average of a group of scores; the sum of all scores divided by the number of scores.

median score refers to the midpoint of a group of scores, that is, the number of scores that are higher equals the number of scores that are lower than the median.

multiple-choice items present a problem (the stem) and several possible responses (options) from which a test-taker is to choose the correct response.

national norms indicate the performance of a sample of all U.S. students at the relevant grade level.

normal curve is the bell shaped symbol showing the approximate distribution of random scores.

norm-referenced scores indicate how a test-taker performs in relation to a specified group of students.

objectives are the intended results of instruction. They should be stated in measurable terms, to permit an assessment of actual performance.

outcomes, like objectives, are the intended, measurable results of instruction.

percentile band indicates a range within which the "true score" falls. It recognizes that every test score is subject to errors of measurement.

percentile rank signifies the score below which a given percent of students in the group falls. A student's percentile rank will vary based on the ability of the norms group with which it is compared.

performance assessment requires that learning be demonstrated by its application to a task.

portfolio assessment refers to an analysis by trained raters of students' work that has been accumulated over time.

rating scales provide categories that allow an observer to indicate the degree of competency an individual demonstrates.

raw score is the number of items answered correctly.

reliability refers to the consistency of results for an assessment instrument, an individual, or a group of test-takers.

scale scores are derived by translating a raw score into a score that uses the normal curve for points of reference. Percentiles are an example of scale scores.

standard deviation indicates how far from the mean the test scores tend to be, that is, whether the scores tend to cluster around the midpoint or are widely dispersed across the score range.

standard error of measurement refers to the extent to which scores would differ if test-takers were retested with a different set of questions that measure the same knowledge and skills at the same level of difficulty.

standard scores describe students' performance on a test in terms of how far a raw score is above or below the mean.

standardized test is an assessment designed to specific content and standards, with detailed procedures for administering and scoring, and which provides normative data for interpreting scores.

stanines (standard nines) are scores distributed over a normal curve with nine scale points or positions. Stanines minimize insignificant differences in scores, as do percentile bands.

subtests are specific samples within a broader domain, for example, vocabulary within the domain of verbal skills. Scores on subtests are usually based on relatively few items, so their reliability is modest.

suburban norms show the achievement of a sample of students in suburban schools.

summative evaluation is a judgment based on the assessment of the overall performance of a program or of individuals in relation to specific objectives.

true score is the hypothetical exact measure of a test-taker's performance. Because every test has some element of measurement error, an exact or true can never be ascertained.

validity means the extent to which an assessment measures what it claims to measure. A measure is valid in relation to the intended use of the assessment results.

Appendix A:
A School Assessment Plan

Assessment, Evaluation, and Accountability
Princeton Charter School
Princeton, New Jersey

INTRODUCTION

On May 29, 1998, the trustees of Princeton Charter School adopted a statement, *Accountability and Improvement*, a description of the school's assessment processes and how they should be used. On adoption by the board, this revised document replaces an earlier statement of board policy.

"Assessment" here simply means the measurement of performance. "Evaluation" refers to judgments or decisions based on the results of assessment. "Accountability" means a full and accurate reporting of a school's policies, operations, and assessment results to all parties of interest.

The Princeton Charter School (PCS) is accountable to its students and their parents, to the staff and board of trustees, to the Princeton Community, and to the State of New Jersey. Each of these constituencies has a right to learn how well the school is carrying out its responsibilities as defined in the school's charter.

Elements covered in this plan:

1. Responsible parties: those who direct the various assessments and evaluations.

2. Subjects: the persons or programs that are assessed and evaluated.
3. Measures: the procedures and instruments for carrying out the assessments and evaluations.
4. Purposes: the rationale and uses for each assessment and evaluation.
5. Schedule: when each process is to be carried out.
6. Reporting: those to whom the results of assessment and evaluation are communicated.

In adopting this plan, the trustees of PCS intend that:

1. The primary purpose of all assessment and evaluation at PCS is the improvement of instruction.
2. All assessments and evaluations of the school will be communicated to the appropriate constituencies, ensuring the transparency that is appropriate for a public school. Only assessment results that are specific to individual students or staff will remain confidential.
3. Results of each assessment will aid in evaluating the results of other assessments; for example, student assessment will clarify the effectiveness of the curriculum and faculty, and vice versa. This integration of assessment results will provide objective data on which to base decisions about curriculum, personnel, etc.

Princeton Charter School holds itself accountable for achieving the following major goals and objectives, as set down in the school's charter.

The principal goals of Princeton Charter School:

1. To educate students for future success.
2. To promote academic excellence and equity for a diverse population of students within a public school system.
3. To provide a choice of educational opportunities within a public school system for parents, students, and educators.

Specific objectives:

1. Students will develop clear and effective written and oral communication skills using standard English.
2. Students will acquire a strong foundation in mathematical reasoning and skills.
3. Students will learn about the political, economic, cultural, geographic, and technological forces that have shaped the history of the world and, specifically, of the United States.
4. Students will acquire knowledge and skills in the sciences and will be able to conduct inquiries using the scientific method.

5. Students will develop an informed appreciation of the arts and participate in their creation.
6. Students will be able to speak, read, and write in a language other than English.
7. Students will learn the essentials necessary for a healthy, safe, and physically fit life.
8. Students will recognize the importance of hard work, personal responsibility, and respect for others.
9. Students from all demographic groups will perform at comparably high achievement levels.

STUDENT ASSESSMENT AND EVALUATION

Classroom Assessment

Teachers are responsible for preparing, administering, and evaluating the results of their student assessments; they also administer standardized examinations in the fall and spring of the school year.

PCS policy requires that teachers evaluate their students by using a variety of assessment measures including brief oral quizzes, written examinations of varying length and complexity, portfolios, homework assignments, and their daily observations of student achievement and behavior. Graded tests and homework assignments should be returned to students with appropriate comments as soon as possible. Teachers are to retain a master copy of their major written tests and assignments for review by their mentors/supervisors and for possible discussion with parents. Teachers' assessments are, cumulatively, the most important and reliable source of information about classes' and individual students' academic progress.

Assigning Grades

In grading student assessments, teachers should:

- Ensure that a single score on a test or assignment does not overly influence a student's quarterly grade. Teachers should set common guidelines for the extent to which tests, classroom participation, homework, and other extra school projects contribute to quarterly grade reports.
- Distinguish between achievement in a subject, for example, mathematics or history, and other factors such as classroom behavior or neatness. For a test score to be valid, it must reflect only what it purports to measure, that is, achievement in the subject tested.

Teachers can use assessment to:

1. Improve instruction through understanding the learning strengths and weaknesses of individuals and groups of students. These insights enable teachers to perceive what needs to be re-taught and the time when students are ready for further learning.
2. Stimulate and focus students' study.
3. Reward student achievement; those who do well receive some recognition or opportunity.
4. Inform students and parents of the status of student learning in relation to the school's standards and the achievement of other students.

Standardized Tests

Standardized tests are administered in the fall for grades three to eight. Since its inception, PCS has used the Educational Records Bureau (ERB) Comprehensive Testing Program (CTP). These examinations focus on verbal skills (reading, writing, listening) and mathematical skills (including mathematical comprehension and reasoning). Teachers administer the CTP and receive scores for their individual students and their classes, as well as item analyses that show how individual students and classes responded to each item on the tests. Parents receive CTP reports for their own children and are invited to make an appointment with a PCS administrator or teacher to discuss the standardized scores in a context of all information concerning their children's progress.

Like all New Jersey public schools, PCS administers the state examinations and, to the extent the timing of the tests and the information in the reports allow, follows the procedure described above for the ERB-CTP.

The role of teachers in standardized testing at PCS includes:

1. Preparing students for the examinations. This preparation should ensure that students are familiar with the directions and item types that will appear on the tests. Of course, students may not be exposed to any questions that will actually appear on the tests. Teachers should encourage students to do their best on standardized tests, as they are an important set of measures that help parents, teachers, and the students themselves perceive what they have learned and what needs to be taught. But teachers must be careful not to overemphasize the importance or accuracy of any single test's results.
2. Evaluating the results of the examinations. Students' scores on standardized tests are primarily a means of confirming and expanding the information from teachers' own assessments. If scores on standardized measures of knowledge and skills differ significantly from a

teacher's own assessment and evaluation, the standardized tests should be checked for alignment of content with the teacher's syllabus. If the standardized measure and the classroom curriculum are not in reasonable conformity, either the standardized measure or the teacher's curriculum should be changed.

In spring, teachers administer the examinations common to all New Jersey public schools. The New Jersey tests are the only measures that allow direct comparisons between PCS students and those in other public schools in the State.

Administrators have several obligations for student assessment:

1. Periodically, they review classroom assessment procedures to ensure that teachers are focusing on important learning objectives and are staying reasonably close to the scheduled course of study.
2. Administrators also regularly schedule in-service teacher activities for designing and using a variety of assessment techniques.
3. Administrators evaluate the results of standardized testing to determine how the school and individual classes are achieving in relation to the test norms; they discuss these results with classroom teachers, and report their conclusions to the Board of Trustees.

Trustees receive an analysis in January of the results of the CTP examinations administered in fall. The Head of School presents his evaluation of the schoolwide and individual classes' scores, and indicates any actions he and other faculty members are taking in response to the score reports. Board members focus especially on evidence of student growth; gains are analyzed by subgroups, especially the highest- and lowest-scoring quartiles of students.

Parents also have a responsibility for the assessment and evaluation of their children's progress. An intimate knowledge of their own children allows them to contribute to evaluating assessment results, homework assignments, and academic grades, as well as the behavior teachers observe in school. Parents can directly assist their children's learning and the ability to demonstrate that learning by ensuring that homework is done carefully and punctually, and by encouraging students to prepare for and do their best on classroom and standardized tests. But parents (and teachers) should not engender excessive anxiety by overemphasizing the significance of any single measure of achievement.

Students are arguably more responsible than anyone for their own assessment and evaluation. It is important that parents and teachers encourage students to accept responsibility for their learning and for evidence of that learning as it is presented through assessment. Not every student can lead the class, but it is an expectation at PCS that all students will progress academically every year. That progress, however, will not be on a perfectly uniform upward curve; it is normal for individual students and entire classes to show learning peaks and valleys over the course of a year.

CURRICULUM ASSESSMENT AND EVALUATION

"Curriculum" is understood to be all the learning activities at PCS. The assessment of curriculum includes a review of:

1. Academic standards and objectives.
2. Instructional content as found in courses of study, lesson plans, texts, etc.
3. Teaching methodologies.
4. Extra-classroom activities, including athletics, social events, etc.

The responsibility for evaluating the curriculum rests ultimately with the Board of Trustees, which must approve any significant changes in the school's programs. PCS's Board depends primarily on recommendations of curriculum committees; for each subject area, a committee of faculty, parents, a board member, and an administrator are joined by at least one subject specialist from outside the school. These committees meet periodically to consider changes in their subject areas; their recommendations are forwarded to the Board for action.

Systematic curriculum review at PCS has several purposes and uses:

1. To determine how well the instructional program works and how it can be improved.
2. To communicate program results to all parties of interest.
3. To ensure systematic development of content within subjects and across grades.
4. To ascertain that human and material resources are sufficient and appropriate for achieving program objectives.

In assessing and evaluating curriculum, PCS committees and the board will pose three questions:

1. Is the program *effective*, that is, does it provide the knowledge, skills, and other outcomes for which the program exists? This question assumes that all programs have measurable objectives and outcomes.
2. Is the program *worth its cost*? School resources, including time, are limited.
3. Does the program enjoy *acceptance*? A committee may be convinced that a program is successful, but if many students, parents, or teachers

oppose it, either those opinions or the program itself should be changed.

TEACHER ASSESSMENT AND EVALUATION

The Head of School and the assistant administrators are responsible for assessing teachers' performance at PCS. Their evaluations of the teaching staff are reported to the Board in closed session at the time contract renewals are under discussion. Teachers are formally evaluated three times yearly, using a standardized form, the Classroom Observation and Teacher Evaluation Report. Teachers discuss the reports with their supervisors and are invited to submit their own comments, which are appended to the reports.

The assessment-evaluation process is both summative and formative in purpose. Summative evaluation is a formal, recorded process that yields a decision, for example, to rehire or give tenure, to reward performance with salary increases, and so on. Formative evaluation is primarily intended to help educators improve; such evaluation can be informal, and often comes most helpfully from one's peers.

Every beginning teacher at PCS is assigned a mentor, a senior staff member who assists the new teacher with lesson plans, classroom management, record keeping requirements, and other typical concerns of beginning teachers. Mentors do not keep written records of those they assist, and they do not contribute to the formal teacher evaluation process. The Head of School may also assign mentors to teachers who need collegial assistance with any aspect of their teaching. Every teacher devises, with a supervisor, a plan for improving content knowledge/teaching strategies. PCS schedules teacher in-service days and allocates funds to each teacher for professional development.

The principal purpose for teacher assessment is the improvement of instruction. Evidence of student learning is the strongest confirmation of good teacher performance. Relating the quality of teaching to student achievement must be done by experienced professional educators with consideration of the many variables that affect student learning. But teachers should regard student learning as the basic purpose and measure of their performance.

ADMINISTRATOR ASSESSMENT AND EVALUATION

At PCS, the Head of School is responsible for assessing the performance of assistant heads and other administrators. That assessment takes place yearly, and the results are conveyed to the Board in closed session. The

Board of Trustees is responsible for assessing and evaluating the Head of School. At the end of the school year, the Chair of the Board meets with the Head of School to discuss the assessment-evaluation results and to explore possible objectives for the following school year.

Systematic evaluation of administrators yields at least two significant benefits at PCS:

1. The evaluation process requires that the school trustees have a clear definition of the administrator's major tasks. The formal agreement of evaluators and those being evaluated on the nature and priorities of the administrator's role reduces misunderstanding and improves trustee–administrator relations.
2. Agreement on the standards by which PCS administrators are assessed means that trustees can fairly and efficiently measure the quality of administrative performance. This process reduces friction, focuses the Board's and the administrator's own expectations, and makes decisions concerning the administrator's future more fair and productive.

BOARD OF TRUSTEES EVALUATION

Parents, faculty, and administrators are constantly assessing informally the effectiveness of the Board and its policies through informal conversations with trustees, most of whom are parents. Board meetings are announced and open to the public, and attendees are invited to comment. The annual survey of parents provides more formal feedback on board policies. Once a year, the Board meets for an entire Saturday at a retreat center to review its stewardship and plans for the future.

ACCOUNTABILITY: A SUMMARY

Princeton Charter School acknowledges the primacy of parents in directing their children's education, so the school is especially accountable to the parents of its students. This obligation requires that the school explain clearly to parents the school's mission and curriculum, and the extent to which school programs are successful for each child and for the entire student body.

PCS shows itself accountable for its academic programs by making available the school's statement of curriculum goals and a description of all of its academic courses.

The activities of the various curriculum committees ensure that the curriculum is known to and approved by faculty, trustees, and parents. School and classwide results of standardized student assessment are distributed to all parents, as are individual student's test results to their parents.

Princeton Charter School uses the results of various assessments to demonstrate the success of its curriculum and teaching to its students, parents, staff, trustees, the Princeton community, and the New Jersey Department of Education. The school's assessment and evaluation processes serve two major purposes: to demonstrate the trustees' intention that the school be accountable for all aspects of its operation, and to assist the school's primary task of teaching and learning.

Revised Policy Adopted: April 13, 2006

Appendix B:
An In-service Program in Assessment

A Workshop on Classroom Assessment

What is the purpose of a workshop on classroom assessment? It is intended to improve the fairness and accuracy of teachers' evaluations of their students, and to achieve that objective by broadening the knowledge, deepening the understanding, and clarifying the attitudes of participants concerning student assessment.

Chapters 3 through 6 of this book deal exclusively with classroom testing, as do some sections of other chapters, especially chapter 2, The Basics of Assessment. We urge the facilitator of this workshop to become thoroughly familiar with that material; even better, workshop participants should be given an opportunity and encouraged to read those chapters as well. But realistically, only a workshop in which all faculty work together on the essentials of classroom assessment is likely to result in significant improvements in assessment practices.

The activities we recommend for a teachers' in-service workshop on classroom assessment can be presented in a workshop of approximately five to six hours. If the facilitator intends to cover standardized tests as well, at least two additional hours are required. We urge that instruction on student assessment not be a one-shot affair. Teachers' understanding of assessment is largely gained through practicing what they have learned, reflecting on the practice, and improving their assessments. In this appendix we recommend sessions to follow the original workshop.

Because facilitators who plan and lead this workshop will be working with professional teachers, they will want to use exemplary teaching methods in conducting the program. We especially urge periods in the program that encourage teachers' comments, recommendations, and questions, as well as small group work, whole group discussion, and other participant activities. The facilitator should suit these and other activities to the experience, needs, and mood of the group.

A FACILITATOR'S PRE-WORKSHOP CHECKLIST

1. As early as possible, provide prospective participants with information in preparation for the workshop:

   - Describe the purpose and planned activities of the workshop.
   - Publicize the arrangements for the workshop: date, time, place, duration, plans for breaks/lunch, materials participants should bring to the workshop. Send reminders shortly before the workshop date.
   - Suggest any preparation or information the participants might find useful to bring to the workshop, for example, samples of their classroom assessments.
   - Ask participants to respond to a brief questionnaire that includes questions about assessment, topics of special interest, problems with grading practices, and so forth. The responses should be submitted to the facilitator at least a week in advance of the workshop.
   - Invite the teachers to bring to the workshop an outline or tentative plan for a test in their subjects.

2. The workshop content outlined here is drawn primarily from the contents of this book; pages in the text are cited for each activity. After the program description in this appendix, we have added several handouts that can be photocopied and distributed to participants. Of course, the training and experience of the facilitator and that of the participants should supplement our recommendations for the workshop.
3. Prepare and test all audio-visual aids: overhead projectors, CDs, and PowerPoint presentations. Prepare handouts, worksheets, and materials for exercises. Additional handouts can be created from the referenced pages in this text.
4. Bring enough supplies for all participants: paper, pencils, and the like.

THE WORKSHOP PROGRAM

We recommend beginning the workshop with refreshments and a few minutes of socializing. The facilitator then reviews the purposes and intended outcomes of the program, and outlines the day's learning activities, the schedule for breaks and lunch, and other important details.

Each activity listed here assumes a fairly brief presentation, often by simply reading the indicated handout, preferably from a projection on a screen. The facilitator should then invite comments and questions. If none are forthcoming, the facilitator should be prepared to pose questions to the group as a whole. At least in the first period of the workshop, individual participants should be called on only if they volunteer.

The abbreviation (HO) means that a handout of the text material referred to should be distributed. The texts for handouts are at the end of this appendix.

We recommend that brief breaks be called at the end of each session, or at least every hour.

FIRST SESSION: PRINCIPLES OF GOOD CLASSROOM ASSESSMENT

Three Basic Qualities and Two Basic Questions of Classroom Assessment

Please refer to chapter 2, pages 31–35, and 37–41 in text (HO 1).

The facilitator explains the principles and gives examples, then requests reactions and classroom applications from the group. We suggest simply reviewing the qualities and questions with the group, then presenting the examples given in chapter 2, or other examples the facilitator or participants can adduce. The facilitator than asks for comments and questions from the group.

This session is an introduction to principles of good classroom assessment. To preserve instructional time for activities that require more participation, we do not recommend a group exercise for this first session.

The facilitator provides a brief summary of the session.

Time for session one: approximately 40 minutes.

SECOND SESSION: PREPARING CLASSROOM TESTS

A. Matching Assessments with Learning Objectives: Student Knowledge and Skills

Please refer to chapter 4, page 59 (HO 2).

Again, the facilitator reviews the handout and offers a few examples of possible test items from several of the taxonomic areas.

Participants are asked to form groups of three to five teachers; as possible, groups should be based on common subjects or grades, that is, math teachers, grade five teachers, and so on. Participants devise and discuss in their groups several assessment items (any type of item) in their subject specialty, using one or more of the learning objectives (HO 2) for each item. Participants keep a written list of the items they have created.

Time for session two, activity A: approximately 45 minutes.

With participants remaining in their small groups, the facilitator introduces the next topic.

B. Item Types

Please refer to chapters 3, 4, 5, and 6 (HO 3).

This is a key section for developing classroom assessment. The handout contains only brief descriptions of the principal item types. The facilitator should supplement those definitions with recommendations for preparing each item type, and indicate the benefits and limitations of each. For this session, the facilitator should be thoroughly familiar with chapters 3 through 6 on item types.

The facilitator asks members in each group to create one or more *selection* items, using the questions they devised in the previous exercise.

After about 10 minutes, or when almost all participants have completed the task, the group moves on to the second item type, *essays*. This exercise requires more time than the preceding one as participants attempt to devise a topic and provide directions for student responses, as the handout prescribes. Participants should also create a restricted essay topic based on the lengthier topic they have just prepared.

The facilitator follows the same procedure for the third major item type, *performance* measures.

When assigning the tasks, the facilitator should encourage the teachers to consult the taxonomy and verbs in HO 2 to create questions that go beyond simple recall of knowledge.

Time for session two, activity B: approximately two hours.

THIRD SESSION:
USING ASSESSMENT FOR STUDENT LEARNING

A. Preparing Students for Major Classroom Tests

Please refer to chapter 2, pages 39–40, (HO 4).

This topic and the one that follows (on using test results) are based on the general principle that assessment should contribute as much as possible to desirable student learning.

With participants remaining in their small groups, the facilitator reads the handout and asks each group to react to the test preparation activities listed in the handout. After a few minutes of discussion within their groups, participants are asked to tell the group as a whole any concerns or disagreement they have with the recommendations from the text. The facilitator summarizes the recommendations and any concerns that have been voiced.

B. Using Results

Refer to chapter 2, pages 40–41, (HO 5).

Participants are asked to follow the same procedure as in activity A. The facilitator again summarizes the recommendations from the text and the comments of participants.

Time for session three, activities A and B: approximately one hour.

Other Topics

Other assessment topics that might be included in this workshop as time allows, or in a future workshop, include standardized tests (see chapter 7) and portfolios (chapter 6, pages 86–89).

Other Activities for Improving Classroom Assessment

- Peer Review of Assessments:

  When teachers prepare a major examination, they want to make it as valid and reliable as possible. Even typos or grammatical errors detract from the quality of the test and give a bad signal to students. More substantively, exam questions and the directions for responding to them should be unambiguous. Whenever possible, teachers should ask a colleague to review their major upcoming examinations a few days before they are administered. This exchange would be an excellent follow-up to the workshop.

- Supervisory Reviews:

  As part of their interest in improving instruction, supervisors should review examinations prepared by their teachers. A major exam indicates the topics a teacher considers most important in his course and the knowledge and skills he expects of his students. Such reviews will be more informative if supervisors receive copies of several corrected and graded examinations.

- Refresher Sessions:

  As mentioned in the introductory section, we strongly recommend brief sessions on classroom assessment during the school year. For semester or end-of-year classroom tests, these reviews are most effective just before and after the tests are prepared.

The workshop handouts that follow are presented on individual pages to facilitate their reproduction for workshop participants. Each handout includes a reference to the pages in the text on which the topic is covered.

HO 1
Basic Qualities and Questions
(Chapter 2, text pages 31–35, 37–41)

The three basic qualities of classroom assessment are:

1. *Validity*, which requires that an assessment measure what it purports to measure; more specifically, validity speaks to how the results of an assessment are used.
2. *Reliability*, which refers to the consistency of assessment results.
3. *Efficiency*, whichrefers to the quality that allows an assessment to yield useful results with the least demand on teachers' and students' time.

The two basic questions teachers should ask as they prepare their assessments are:

1. Why am I giving this assessment? That is, how will the results be used?
2. More specifically, how will I use the process and results of my assessment to further student learning?

HO 2
Levels of Knowledge and Skills
(Chapter 4, text page 59)

In preparing questions and problems for student assessment, teachers can choose the actions words that best assess the cognitive knowledge and skills they are seeking. If a teacher intends to examine:

- *Knowledge:* ask students to identify, list, match, name, recognize, select.
- *Comprehension:* ask them to classify, explain, distinguish, interpret, predict, summarize, understand.
- *Application:* ask students to compute, demonstrate, arrange, adapt, practice, modify, operate, solve.
- *Analysis:* ask them to examine, diagnose, differentiate, diagram, estimate, infer, separate, order.
- *Evaluation:* ask students to criticize, compare, contrast, rate, judge, justify, conclude, support, discriminate.
- *Creativity:* ask them to design, construct, revise, combine, compose, formulate.

HO 3
Types of Formal Assessment Items
(Chapters 3, 4, 5, 6)

This handout refers to "formal" assessment—item types used in written examinations—in contrast to teachers' daily informal observation and questioning of students' achievement.

A necessary prelude to choosing the best types of items for an exam is a decision on how the results will be used. Teachers can assess for at least three purposes:

Formative assessment is intended to inform students and their teachers of what students have learned, and what they need to study next. It can be informal, and is seldom used for assigning student grades or for making decisions about promotion or placement.

Summative assessment yields a "bottom line," a judgment or decision. Standardized state examinations are an example of summative assessment; some teachers heavily weight the results of their end-of-course exams in assigning a grade for the year.

Diagnostic assessment is largely formative in purpose. It focuses on specific learning problems of an individual or small group of students. Results from diagnostic assessment should quickly lead to the remedial instruction indicated by the assessment results. In more extensive diagnoses, results may lead to summative decisions about grade or school placement.

The principal categories of items in classroom assessment are:

1. *Recognition items,* which present students with both questions and answers; the students' task is to choose the best answer from among the options given. Two of the best known types of recognition items are multiple-choice and matching items.
2. *Supply items,* which require that students create their answers. These include short-answer items, and both brief and extended essay questions.
3. *Performance items,* which are work samples: students must perform a task that demonstrates their ability to do so.

HO 4
Preparing Students for Classroom Tests
(Chapter 2, text pages 39–40)

A great deal of classroom assessment is informal, and formative in intent. We refer here to major tests, usually written and at least a full class period in length. Results of these exams often contribute to semester or course grades, and to decisions such as promotion or placement. In addition to those summative purposes, major tests can also contribute to student and teacher learning through focused preparation for and review of their results.

In preparing students for a major examination, teachers can:

- Tell students the type of questions that will appear on the exams, for example, multiple choice, or restricted essays, and remind them of efficient ways of responding to the questions. This should be done several days before the exam.
- Review the important content that will be sampled in the test. Point out key material in the text, students' notes, homework assignments, projects, and so on.
- "Give away" one or a few items on the exam by saying, for example, "One of the following three topics will be a brief essay question."
- Discuss in class efficient ways of preparing for and taking the test. Simple test skills like keeping track of available time or checking answers can yield more valid scores.
- Let students prepare one or more questions for the test and discuss appropriate responses. If everyone has an excellent answer on the exam, all students, especially the lower achieving ones, will be encouraged.
- Communicate a desire and an expectation that every student will do well on the test.

HO 5
Using the Results of Classroom Tests
(Chapter 2, text pages 40–41)

Students can derive considerable instructional benefit from tests when teachers observe a few procedures following the test administration:

- Score tests, as well as homework and projects, and review them in class as soon as possible. Prompt attention to students' work can reinforce desirable learning and prevent errors from becoming entrenched through repetition.
- Take time in class to review assessment results, especially those from major tests. Place the questions and responses in the context of the course: Why is this question important? How does each question relate to earlier learning or to what lies ahead?
- Use student deficiencies on an exam question as remediation exercises on a homework assignment.
- Learn from the results of the assessments. If many students, especially the higher achievers, missed a question, ask, "Why?" Was the question ambiguous? Did I cover the material adequately in class? Should I re-teach some of this material, perhaps using a different teaching strategy?

References and Bibliography

American Educational Research Association. (2007). www.aeva.net.

American Educational Research Association, American Psychological Association, and National Council on Measurement in Education. (1999). *Standards for educational and psychological testing*. Washington, DC: American Educational Research Association.

American Evaluation Association. (n.d.). [Services menu]. Retrieved November 4, 2007, from www.eval.org.

Anderson, L. W., & Krathwohl, D. R. (Eds.). (2001). *A taxonomy for learning, teaching, and assessing: A revision of Bloom's taxonomy of educational objectives* (Complete ed.). Boston: Allyn & Bacon.

Arasian, P. W. (2001). *Classroom assessment* (4th ed.). New York: McGraw-Hill.

Barton, P. E. (2004). *Unfinished business: More measured approaches in standards-based reform*. Princeton, NJ: Educational Testing Service.

Bereiter, C., & Engelmann, S. (1966). *Teaching disadvantaged children in the preschool*. Englewood Cliffs, NJ: Prentice-Hall.

Bloom, B. S. (Ed.). (1956). *Taxonomy of educational objectives: The classification of educational goals*. Handbook 1: *Cognitive domain*. New York: David McKay.

Bolick, C. (2006, July 12). Remedial education. *The Wall Street Journal*, p. A16.

Bosman, J. (2007, May 31). City expands test program in schools. *The New York Times*, pp. B1, B2.

Broad Foundation. (2007). *The Broad Prize for urban education—press kit*. [See also Past Winners.] Retrieved November 20, 2007, from www.BroadPrize.org.

Brown, Henry. (2000). *Using student progress to evaluate teachers: A primer on value-added models*. Princeton, NJ: Educational Testing Service.

Capps, F. C. (n.d.). *Review: Eric clearinghouse on assessment and evaluation: ericae.net*. Retrieved November 15, 2007, from Google search for Eric clearinghouse on assessment and evaluation ericae.net. [See also www.ericae.net.]

Center for American Progress and Institute for America's Future. (2005). *Getting smarter, becoming fairer: A progressive education agenda for a stronger nation.* Washington, DC: Author.

Center on Education Policy. (2006, March). *From the Capital to the classroom: Year 4 of the No Child Left Behind Act.* Washington, DC: Author.

Davies, G. K. (2006). *Setting a public agenda for higher education in the United States: Lessons learned from the National Collaborative for Higher Education Policy.* San Jose, CA: National Collaborative for Higher Education.

Davis, M. R. (2007). Texas hold'em: Secretary Spellings—the ace in Bush's hand. *Education Next, 7*(3), 13–17.

Deneen, J. R., & Deneen, C. C. (2005). *A board's guide to assessment in the school: Understanding roles and methods.* Washington, DC: National Catholic Educational Association.

Dillon, S. (2005, November 26). Students ace state tests, but earn "Ds" from U.S. *The New York Times,* pp. A1, A12.

Dillon, S. (2006, March 26). Schools cut back subjects to push reading and math. *The New York Times,* pp. A1, A22.

Duckworth, A. L., & Seligman, M. E. P. (2005). Self-discipline outdoes IQ in predicting academic performance in adolescents. *Psychological Science, 16*(12), 939–944.

Education Commission of the States. (2004, July). *ECS Report to the Nation: State Implementation of the No Child Left Behind Act* (Report cards: Indicator 6) [Electronic pdf version]. (Education Commission of the States Distribution Center No. GP-04-01). Retrieved November 10, 2007, from www.ecs.org/NCLB [sic].

Education Trust. (2005). *Gaining traction, gaining ground: How some high schools accelerate learning for struggling students.* Washington, DC: Author.

Elmont Memorial Junior-Senior High School. (2006). Elmont Memorial High School, Nassau County New York [2001–2006 scores and rankings]. [Review by] Karen Chenoweth. (2006, April 20). *Much better than adequate progress.* Retrieved November 18, 2007, from www.achievementalliance.org/files/Elmont pdf [sic].

Esquith, R. (2007). *Teach like your hair's on fire: The method and madness inside room 56.* New York: Viking.

Evers, W. M., & Walberg, H. J. (Eds.). (2004). *Testing student learning, evaluating teacher effectiveness.* Stanford, CA: Hoover Institution Press.

Fuller, T. (Ed.). (1989). *The voice of liberal learning: Michael Oakeshott on education.* New Haven and New London: Yale University Press.

Gootman, E. (2007, October 18). Teachers agree to bonus pay tied to scores. *The New York Times,* pp. A1, B6.

Greene, J. P., & Forster, G. (2003, September). *Public high school graduation and college readiness rates in the United States* (Education Working Paper No. 3). New York: Manhattan Institute for Policy Research.

Greene, J. P., & Winters, M. A. (2006). The effects of residential school choice on public high school graduation rates. *Peabody Journal of Education, 81*(1), 203–216.

Gronlund, N. E. (2006). *Assessment of student achievement* (8th ed.). Upper Saddle River, NJ: Pearson Education.

Harvard University School of Education. (2007). *Arts PROPEL* [Updated]. Retrieved November 10, 2007, from www.pz.harvard.edu/Research/PROPEL.htm.

Henderson, H. (2006). *Let's kill Dick and Jane: How the Open Court Publishing Company fought the culture of American education.* South Bend, IN: St. Augustine Press.

Herbert, R. (2005, August 29). Left behind, way behind. *The New York Times,* p. A15.

Hess, F. M., & Petrilli, M. J. (2006). *No child left behind.* New York: Peter Lang.

Hirsch, E. D., Jr. (1987). *Cultural literacy: What every American needs to know.* Boston: Houghton Mifflin.

Hirsch, E. D., Jr. (2006). *The knowledge deficit: Closing the shocking education gap for American children.* Boston: Houghton Mifflin.

Human Resources Research Organization. (2007, October). *Behind the numbers: Interviews in 22 states about achievement data and No Child Left Behind Act policies* (Phase 2 Report). Washington, DC: Center on Education Policy. Retrieved January 5, 2008, from No Child Left Behind at www.cep-dc.org.

Krueger, A. B., Hanushek, E. A., & Rice, J. K. (Contributors). (2002). In L. Mishel & R. Rothstein (Eds.), *The class size debate.* Washington, DC: Economic Policy Institute.

Lareau, A. (2003). *Unequal childhood, class, race, and family life.* Berkeley: University of California Press.

Lewin, T. (2007, June 8). States found to vary widely on education. *The New York Times,* p. A21.

Lindsey, B. (2007, July 9). The culture gap. *The Wall Street Journal,* p. A15.

Linn, R. L., & Gronlund, N. E. (2000). *Measurement and assessment in teaching* (8th ed.). Upper Saddle River, NJ: Merrill-Prentice Hall.

McCaffrey, D. F., Koretz, D., Lockwood, J. R., & Hamilton, L. S. (2004). *Evaluating value-added models for teacher accountability.* Retrieved November 20, 2007, from Browse by Author name at www.rand.org/pubs/authors.

Medina, J. (2007, September 19). New York schools win award for achievement. *The New York Times,* p. B6.

National Assessment of Educational Progress. (2007). NAEP high school transcript study subject area. *America's high school graduates: Results from the 2005 NAEP high school transcript study* [Electronic version]. Retrieved November 4, 2007, from www.nces.ed.gov/nationsreportcard/hsts.

National Association of State Boards of Education. (2005, October). *Evaluating value-added: Findings and recommendations from the NASBE Study Group on Value-Added Assessments.* Alexandria, VA: Author.

New Jersey Department of Education. (2007). *Review report January 8–12, 2007.* Retrieved November 8, 2007, from www.ed.gov/admins/lead/account/monitoring/reports07/njrpt.doc. [Web address changes often; also available from New Jersey State Library, New Jersey Collections, and their online Library Catalog, New Jersey Docs Call Number 974.90 E24 2007a; electronic copy available.]

North Central Regional Educational Laboratory. (1999). *Critical issue: Assessing young children's progress appropriately* (By Tynette W. Hills, posted 1997; rev. 1999). Retrieved November 18, 2007, from www.ncrel.org/sdrs/areas/issues/students/earlycld/ea500.htm.

North Star Academy Charter School. (1997–2006). Our Results. Retrieved November 14, 2007, from www.northstaracademy.org.

Noteboom, J.T., Barnholt, K. R., & Enoka, R. M. (2001). Activation of the arousal response and impairment of performance increase with anxiety and stressor intensity. *Journal of Applied Physiology, 91,* 2093–2101.

Oosterhoff, A. C. (2000). *Classroom applications of educational measurement* (3rd ed.). Upper Saddle River, NJ: Merrill-Prentice Hall.

Peterson, P. E., & Hess, F. M. (2006). Keeping an eye on state standards: A race to the bottom? *Education Next, 6*(3), 28–29.

Popham, W. J. (2005). *Classroom assessment: What teachers need to know* (4th ed.). Boston: Pearson Education.

Princeton Charter School. (2007). Princeton Charter School—Site Index. Retrieved November 15, 2007, from www.pcs.k12.nj.us.

Project STAR. (1999). *The Tennessee student/teacher achievement ratio study: Background & 1999 update.* Retrieved November 8, 2007, from www.heros-inc.org/star99.pdf.

Rumberger, R. W., & Larson, K. A. (1998). Student mobility and the increased risk of high school dropout. *American Journal of Education, 107*(1), 1–35.

Saulny, S. (2005, January 19). State to state: Varied ideas of "Proficient." *The New York Times,* p. B8.

Schemo, D. J. (2006, August 23). Study of test scores finds charter schools lagging. *The New York Times,* p. A14.

Stiggins, R. L. (2004). *Assessment for student learning: Doing it right, using it well.* Princeton, NJ: Educational Testing Service Assessment Training Institute.

Tomsho, R. (2005, December 2). How Charlotte tops big cities in school tests. *The Wall Street Journal,* pp. B1, B2.

Tomsho, R. (2006, March 23). More districts pay teachers for performance. *The Wall Street Journal,* pp. B1, B5.

Tomsho, R. (2007, February 23). Report raises questions about high school courses. *The Wall Street Journal,* pp. B1, B2.

U.S. Department of Education Office of Innovation and Improvement. (2006, October). *Charter high schools: Closing the achievement gap. Innovations in education* (North Star Academy) [Electronic version]. (U.S. Department of Education Contract No. ED-01-CO-0012, Task Order D010, prepared by WestEd). Retrieved November 10, 2007, from www.ed.gov/admins/comm/choice/charterhs/report.pdf.

U.S. General Accounting Office. (1994). *Elementary school children: Many change schools frequently, harming their education* (ERIC Document Reproduction Service No. ED 369 526). Washington, DC: Author.

Weingarten, R. (2007, March 18). What matters most: Using student test scores to evaluate teachers: Common sense or nonsense? [Microfilm]. *The New York Times,* p. WK 5.

Weingarten, R. (2007, April 15). What matters most: Does it count? [Microfilm]. *The New York Times,* p. WK 5.

Wortham, S. C. (2005). *Assessment in early childhood education* (4th ed.). Upper Saddle River, NJ: Pearson Education.

About the Authors

Christopher Deneen is assistant dean for academic affairs and an associate professor in the Graduate School of Education and Psychology at Touro College in New York City. He teaches courses in the assessment of general and special education curricula, and in social studies. Chris chairs the Graduate School's Committee on Institutional Assessment; he also mentors teachers in New York's public schools. Chris was a middle and high school teacher and department chair of social studies at All Saints Academy in Winter Haven, Florida. He has published in the areas of curriculum and assessment and presented at meetings of the American Educational Research Association and the National Council for Social Studies. Chris holds a doctorate in curriculum and teaching from Teachers College, Columbia University, and a master of arts in teaching from Indiana University.

James Deneen is retired from Educational Testing Service, where he was a director for the Advanced Placement Program and for Teacher Programs and Services. Earlier, he was a teacher and school administrator, and taught school administration at the University of Toronto's Graduate School of Education. He has written some forty books and articles, principally on educational assessment, and has presented numerous workshops on that topic. He also coauthored with Chris Deneen a self-assessment program and a text on assessment for school boards. Jim received his doctorate in educational administration from Indiana University.